CELEBRATED
CITIZENS
of BELFAST

In association with Belfast City Council

CELEBRATED CITIZENS of BELFAST

John Bradbury

Appletree Press

First published in 2002 by
Appletree Press Ltd
The Old Potato Station
14 Howard Street South
Belfast
BT7 1AP

Tel: (0) 28 90 243074
Fax: (0) 28 90 246756
E-mail: reception@appletree.ie
Web Site: www.appletree.ie

A catalogue record for this book is available from the British Library.

Celebrated Citizens of Belfast

ISBN 0-86281-834-6

Commissioning & General Editor: Paul Harron
Designer: Wayne Matier

In association with Belfast City Council
www.belfastcity.gov.uk/heritage

Front cover illustrations (clockwise from top left): James Young; Sir Edward Harland;
Sister Genevieve; George Best; Brian Kennedy; Henry Joy McCracken; Marie Jones;
Sir Arthur Chichester; Ruby Murray; John Boyd Dunlop (centre)
Title page illustration: *The Reading of the Belfast Town Charter* mural by John Luke, 1951,
Belfast City Hall dome (Photographic credits on p96)

CONTENTS

Foreword

I am delighted to introduce *Celebrated Citizens of Belfast*, the first ever book dedicated to the famous citizens of Belfast. As our city bids to become European Capital of Culture 2008, Belfast City Council is proud to contribute to the celebration of the visionaries, entrepreneurs, and creative thinkers who helped lay the foundations of today's Belfast, the 'Renaissance City'.

I believe this book is a timely reminder of the people that make up the Belfast story. Many of the names to be found here represent achievements of which all citizens of Belfast can be justifiably proud.

I also offer this book to Belfast's visitors, as a record of this diverse and vibrant city, inhabited by talented, and, in many cases, internationally renowned people, to whom all of us can turn, and return, for inspiration.

The Right Honourable
The Lord Mayor, Councillor Jim Rodgers
March 2002

Introduction

This book was conceived by Belfast City Council's Development (Arts) Sub-Committee to provide an enlightening introduction to *some* of the many remarkable characters who have called Belfast 'home'. The resulting selection of brief biographies forms a panoply of inspiring figures, past and present, from all walks of life and parts of the city.

Our criteria for inclusion were that each person had a real bond with Belfast and had spent a significant or formative period in it. The majority were born in the city; however, we have also included those born elsewhere but who lived, worked, were educated or died here and could reasonably be thought of as Belfast citizens. Generally speaking, these celebrated sons and daughters of the city contributed directly to the life of Belfast, but we have also aimed to include those whose contributions have made an impact elsewhere around the world.

Due to limitations of space, it has proved impossible to include everyone we would have liked to feature. Belfast has produced such a huge crop of talented and fascinating citizens that we had to make some very difficult editorial decisions. Readers should think of this book as an inspirational 'taster', not a definitive or exhaustive list. In many cases, especially contemporary entries, a biography should be seen as representative of a whole area of life in which several other significant people play or played key roles.

In this period of rapid political transition, the writing of history is complex and contentious. When it came to recent or current Belfast politicians we felt that we should not seek to influence posterity, accidentally or otherwise. We therefore adopted a policy of only including someone who was born 100 or more years ago or who had been dead for at least 20 years. This decision has not, however, meant that the book is without its bold and controversial figures.

Where possible, each biography includes references to other notable characters and also associated physical sites in the city – from where a subject lived or worked, to, in some instances, a commemorative plaque or public monument. Cross-references are highlighted in CAPITAL LETTERS and make for intriguing points of connection. Entries are given alphabetically by surname and each person is listed under the name by which most people knew them – so professional titles (Doctor, Professor, Archbishop etc.) and titular styles (such as Sir or Lord) are only included where it significantly aids identification; we have aimed to include mention of any honours in the body of the text if not given in the heading.

It is hoped that this compilation will encourage readers to discover new associations with people and places around the city and be reminded of old ones, and to think afresh about some of the dynamic citizens who make up the living history of Belfast, the city which in the words of John Hewitt '…drew the landless in, that river-straddling, hill-rimmed town'.

Paul Harron
General Editor

PATRICK ADAIR *(c. 1620–94)* | Presbyterian Minister and Author

Patrick Adair was a major figure in seventeenth-century Presbyterianism, and was instrumental in the establishment of the Presbyterian Church in the north of Ireland.

Born in Greenock in Scotland, Adair was one of a group of young Scottish Presbyterian ministers who travelled over to Ireland in the 1640s. In 1646, he was ordained at Cairncastle, near Larne. During 1648, he was on a committee with Generals Monk and Coote in Belfast to establish Presbyterianism. When Charles I was beheaded in 1649, Adair was amongst protesting ministers praying for the re-establishment of the monarchy under Charles II, who promised to establish Presbyterianism in the north.

Adair acted as spokesman, on behalf of the Presbytery, declining to accept the Commonwealth under Oliver Cromwell. He was also one of two ministers appointed to meet with General Fleetwood in Dublin in 1652, a meeting which ended in frustration. Adair returned north and, unable to find shelter among local people because of his religion, had to hide amongst the rocks near Cairncastle. Two years later Adair was back in Dublin, lobbying for tithes and annual salaries for Presbyterian ministers.

Further frustration ensued for Adair during the 1660s, although eventually a meeting house was constructed for him at Cairncastle in 1668. Adair engaged in further negotiations to improve the lot of Presbyterians in the 1670s. In 1674 he was appointed as a minister in First Presbyterian Church, Rosemary Street in Belfast, but the Donegall family – Belfast's powerful leading family (see SIR ARTHUR CHICHESTER) – disapproved, preferring English Presbyterianism over its Scottish counterpart. Controversy and conflict persisted until James II gave Presbyterians renewed liberty in 1687. There was, however, no Irish Toleration Act until 1719.

In 1689, Adair led a deputation from the General Committee of Ulster Presbyterians to see William III in London. The King appointed Adair as one of the trustees for distributing money to Presbyterians, through the 'regium donum', granted to Adair and other Presbyterians at Hillsborough in 1690.

Adair continued to strive for Presbyterian freedom for the rest of his life, and he published *A True Narrative of the Rise and Progress of the Presbyterian Government in the North of Ireland*. He married twice – first to his first cousin, Jean, a daughter of Sir Robert Adair of Ballymena, and after her death, to Elizabeth Anderson. He had four sons and one daughter. Two of his sons, William and Patrick, also became ministers. A copy of Adair's will is displayed in the Rosemary Street church.

FRED ALDERDICE *(1872–1936)* | Prime Minister of Newfoundland

Born in Belfast on 10th November 1872, Fred Alderdice was Prime Minister of Newfoundland during the late 1920s and again from 1932 until 1934. He was related to the Munros of Lisburn/Moira, who boast Henry Munro, leader of the United Irishmen in Co. Down, as their ancestor. (Henry Munro was hanged outside his shop in Lisburn in 1798; his widow, a friend of MARY ANN MCCRACKEN lived in Chichester Street in Belfast.)

Alderdice was educated at Methodist College, Belfast. He left Belfast in the late 1880s and emigrated to Newfoundland, Canada, where he became a successful businessman. He was a director of a number of concerns including Newfoundland Manufacturers Mutual Insurance Company, Newfoundland Hotel Limited and Newfoundland Motor Mutual Insurance Association.

Gravitating towards politics, Alderdice became the Commissioner for Home Affairs and Education in Newfoundland. In 1924, he was voted a member of the Legislative Council for the Province and rose to become Prime Minister in August 1928.

Alderdice lost power in November 1928, but returned as Prime Minister from June 1932 until January 1934. He died at St John's, Newfoundland on 23rd February 1936.

THOMAS ANDREWS *(1813–85)* | Chemist

Doctor Thomas Andrews is recognised internationally for his chemistry research. He investigated ozone and the continuity of liquid and gaseous states (his work was to eventually lead to inventions like the refrigerator), and he was the first scientist to establish that ozone is not a compound but is oxygen in an altered form. Andrews also carried out exhaustive research on thermodynamics.

Andrews was born in Belfast on 19th December 1813 and educated at the Belfast Academical Institution ('Inst.' – later the Royal Belfast Academical Institution). He later studied in Dublin, Glasgow, and Edinburgh, where he qualified as a Doctor of Medicine. In 1835 he worked in Paris under Dumas, the eminent chemist. Returning to Belfast, he taught for eleven years at Inst. while also establishing a medical practice. Appointed Professor of Chemistry at Queen's College, Andrews established the School of Medicine at the College in 1849 and was later appointed Vice President of the College.

Andrews held numerous honorary positions, including Honorary Fellow of the Royal Society of Edinburgh and President of the British Association for the Advancement of Science in 1876. He declined a knighthood in 1880. He had many other interests besides science. He was a member of the Royal Irish Academy and also of the Belfast Natural History and Philosophical Society. Andrews published many pamphlets including *The Church in Ireland* (1869), in which he argued for the disestablishment of the Anglican Church of Ireland and the distribution of its assets.

He died on 26th November 1885 at Fortwilliam Park, North Belfast. Queen's students presented his portrait to the College and a chemistry studentship was set up in his name.

WILLIAM *(1824–86)* **and GEORGE BAIRD** *(1833–75)* | Founders of the *Belfast Evening Telegraph*

Brothers William and George Baird were responsible for the inception of the *Belfast Evening Telegraph* (now the *Belfast Telegraph*), first published on 1st September 1870, and Ireland's first halfpenny newspaper.

William Savage Baird was born on 9th September 1824 in Randalstown. Aged 14, he was apprenticed to the office of *The Ulster Times*, edited by Isaac Butt (founder of the Home Rule League). He worked hard, passed his printing exams and worked for a couple of other publishers before landing a job as Manager of the Printing Department of *The Belfast Mercury*, which was published by the Ulster Printing Company based at 10–12 Arthur Street. Baird had a reputation for being a workaholic. Married to Margaret Jane Canning, they had five children and lived at 1 Cromac Park Terrace, now 149 Ormeau Road. He was a staunch Conservative and a member of the Orange Order.

His brother George Courtenay Baird was born in 1833. Known for his shrewdness and caution in business, he was an overseer in the Printing Department of *The Daily Mercury*, also printed at 10–12 Arthur Street. In 1861, the Bairds bought the building, plant and goodwill of the Ulster Printing Company for £450. For years they lucratively printed pamphlets on contract to various local railways and for the Provincial Bank of Ireland.

Their plans to start *The Belfast Daily Mail* fell through, but it wasn't long before they started their biggest venture. William happened to be walking home with his son when he saw a billboard declaring *The Evening Press* would publish its first edition on 6th September 1870. His mind was made up to start an evening newspaper. On 1st September 1870, the

Belfast Evening Telegraph was published and cost a halfpenny. A four-page issue, it covered the Franco-Prussian War and local news. The Bairds organised an elaborate launch to attract publicity. Sales exceeded expectations and in November 1870 they ordered a new press to treble capacity. At the time there were only five other evening newspapers in Britain.

The newspaper flourished. George Baird died in 1875, but William continued to hold the reins. In the early 1880s, he moved the newspaper to its current site on Royal Avenue. William Baird died in 1886. Determined businessmen, the brothers built up a part of Belfast life that lives on.

JAMES CAMLIN BECKETT *(1912–96)* | Historian

Professor J.C. Beckett was a renowned Irish historian and writer of international repute who also became the first Professor of History at Queen's University. Born in Belfast in 1912, he was educated at the Royal Belfast Academical Institution ('Inst.') and at Queen's. He went on to lecture at Queen's and held the position of Professor from 1958 until 1975. Beckett was also a Member of the Royal Commission on Historical manuscripts from 1960 until 1986. He received honorary degrees from the University of Ulster and Queen's.

Beckett's accessible approach to history is evident in his many books which included *A Short History of Ireland 1603–1923* (1956), *The Making of Modern Ireland* (1966) and *Belfast, The Making of the City* (1983). He died in a Belfast nursing home on 12th February 1996.

Belfast boasts other historical writers of considerable note. Theodore William Moody lectured at Queen's and was Professor of Modern History at Trinity College Dublin from 1940 until 1977. Born in Belfast in 1907, Moody was also educated at Inst. and Queen's. His lecturing and professorship aside, Moody founded *The Journal of Irish Historical Studies* and is remembered for *The Course of Irish History* edited together with Professor F.X. Martin. Arguably his greatest work was *Davitt and the Irish Revolution*. Moody died in Dublin on 11th February 1984.

Overlapping with Moody at Trinity was Belfast-born eminent historian Professor R.B. McDowell. Educated at Inst. and Trinity, he lectured in Dublin for many years. He has written several books, including *Crisis and Decline*, about Unionism in the Republic. McDowell was remembered at Trinity as a lecturer of flair matched with eccentricity.

JOHN STUART BELL *(1928–90)* | Nuclear Physicist

John Bell was a nuclear physicist who produced a series of experiments and papers on elementary particle physics, quantum mechanics, and nuclear theory. He is best remembered for his equation 'Bell's Inequalities' which was proof of Quantum Theory.

Bell was born in South Belfast in 1928. He was educated at Old Ulsterville Elementary School, Fane Street Secondary School and the Belfast Technical College. He started work aged 16 as a laboratory assistant in the Physics Department at Queen's University. His potential was soon recognised and he took a degree in Theoretical Physics. He continued his studies at Trinity College, Dublin and Birmingham University, where he discovered an important theory involving symmetry in physics.

In 1949, Bell moved to work at the Atomic Energy Research Establishment at Harwell, England. In 1960, he moved to CERN, a nuclear research centre at Geneva. Bell's experiments proved how measurements on one proton would affect measurements on the other.

Bell often returned to Northern Ireland to visit his family and give lectures. He received numerous honours, including recognition from the American Academy of Arts and Science. He died at home in Geneva aged only 62 after suffering a brain haemorrage. He left a wife, May, and was survived by his parents who lived in Tate's Avenue, as well as his brothers David and Robert and sister Ruby. At the time of Bell's death in 1990, his brother Robert was a professor of electronics in Canada.

GEORGE BENN (1801–82) | Belfast Historian and Hospital Founder

George Benn was born in Tandragee, Co. Armagh in 1801 but went on to become a pupil at Belfast Academy and the Belfast Academical Institution.

In 1819, whilst still at school, he published an essay entitled 'A History of Belfast'. The work came to the attention of *News Letter* editor James McKnight, who published it. Benn won a prize for the essay, but he spent most of his working life as a distiller in Downpatrick and later as a distiller and farmer on the family estate at Glenravel, Ballymena.

Benn worked alongside his brother Edward, who in the 1830s purchased the large tract of land at Glenravel. Edward built Glenravel House and developed iron ore deposits so successfully that the family amassed a vast amount of wealth.

Together George and Edward were responsible for establishing three hospitals in Belfast – the Samaritan Hospital, the Hospital for Diseases of the Skin and the Benn Ulster Eye, Ear and Throat Hospital. Edward Benn founded the hospitals and George was the benefactor.

George Benn was asked to complete his history of Belfast, but modestly proposed that the work be entrusted to William Pinkerton. When Pinkerton died, Benn decided to write two volumes of history, the first of which is introduced with the words 'It's my own work from beginning to end'. Benn completed the two volumes, the second of which covers 1799 to 1819. The complete work is entitled *A History of the Town of Belfast from the Earliest Times to the Close of the Eighteenth Century*.

Edward Benn also paid for two extensions to the Poor House in North Queen Street. His collection of Irish antiquities, the largest private collection in Northern Ireland, was donated to the Belfast Museum in College Square North in 1879 (they are now in the Ulster Museum in Stranmillis). Edward died in 1874 and was buried in Clifton Street Graveyard.

George Benn's works were published in 1877/80 and he died on 8th January 1882. Both brothers were unmarried and were survived by four sisters.

GEORGE BEST (1946–) | Footballer

George Best, one of the most talented players to grace a football pitch anywhere in the history of the game, grew up in the Cregagh district of Belfast. He passed his eleven plus, but was so keen on soccer that he left grammar school because rugby dominated the sporting curriculum. Although overlooked by local clubs, Manchester United's chief scout Bob Bishop noted his talent and recommended Best for an apprenticeship at the age of 15. After some deliberation, Best took the boat to England along with Eric McMordie (who later made his name with Middlesborough).

In September 1963, aged 17, Best made his debut for Manchester United against West Bromwich Albion. Best established himself with some inspired performances – United reached the semi-finals of the F.A. Cup before losing to eventual winners West Ham United.

In May 1964, Best made his debut for Northern Ireland (for which he was to be capped 37 times) against Wales, just after his 18th birthday. The next few years witnessed Best's mercurial rise to become a household name. United won the League the following year, and Best, alongside Law and Bobby Charlton, received the plaudits. In 1965 United destroyed star-studded Benfica of Lisbon in the European Cup. Best was magnificent; both scoring and setting up goals. The local press called him 'El Beatle' because of his long hair.

Manchester United won the League again in 1967, and qualified for the European Cup. By mid-autumn, the team was already top of the League. Playing for Northern Ireland against

Manchester United footballer George Best photographed outside one of his boutiques, 1970

Scotland, Best also produced a winning display at Windsor Park. By now, Best was constantly in the public eye and on the back page of all the newspapers. A series of superb performances in 1967/8 helped put Manchester United on top of the First Division and in the semi-finals of the European Cup again. A brilliant comeback in Madrid and a scintillating extra time display against Benfica in the final saw Manchester United win the European Cup, succeeding Glasgow Celtic. Best was voted 1968 English and European Footballer of the Year.

When Matt Busby retired as Manchester United's manager, the team declined and although Best still turned in some brilliant displays, the old consistency had gone. Despite some inspired play in the early 1970s, the team lost patience with the erratic genius in 1973.

For the next ten years, Best became a soccer nomad. A reasonably productive time at Second Division Fulham was followed by his £1,000-per-game phase for Hibernian. He played in America for a while, most notably for the Los Angeles Aztecs. His English League career wound up with Bournemouth in 1983.

Best's health has caused him problems in recent years. He came back to Northern Ireland to live for a while with his wife in Portavogie, Co. Down, before deciding to return to live in London.

Best's footballing career was summed up by the famous Brazilian footballer Pelé, who described him as the greatest footballer in the world.

JOSEPH GILLIS BIGGAR *(1828–90)* | Nationalist Politician

Born in Belfast in 1828, Joseph Gillis Biggar was famous for his obstructionist tactics in the House of Commons. Biggar was educated at Belfast Academy, and then went to work in his father's provisions business in Belfast, taking over the firm in 1861. Life as a successful merchant did not satisfy him, and he became active in Nationalist politics. He was elected as Member of Parliament for Cavan in 1874, and remained in the House of Commons until his death in 1890. In Belfast, he lived at 88 Donegall Street (where Home Rule League leader Charles Stewart Parnell was a visitor) and had business premises at 9–11 Henry Street.

Biggar was treasurer of the Land League and was a member of the Irish Republican Brotherhood Supreme Council from 1875 to 1877. The Council transacted its business on House of Commons' notepaper! In 1877, Biggar, originally a Presbyterian, converted to Catholicism.

Due to the 1850 Franchise Act, the number of Nationalist MPs increased because more people had the vote in Ireland. Armed with 85 members, Biggar and fellow MP Isaac Butt (founder of the Home Rule movement) were able to obstruct the progress of business in the House – a ruse designed to improve Home Rule opportunity, and which was later successfully employed by Parnell.

Outspoken and abrasive (and noted for a Belfast accent which fellow MPs found hard to understand), Biggar wasn't afraid of letting others know his opinion. At times Isaac Butt found his manner and techniques off-putting, but Biggar's contribution to 19th-century Nationalist politics was considerable. He died on 19th February 1890 in London and was buried in Belfast.

FRANCIS JOSEPH BIGGER *(1863–1926)* | Author and Antiquary

Francis Joseph Bigger was devoted to the study of Irish archaeology, local history and the Irish language. Born in Belfast in 1863, Bigger was educated at the Royal Belfast Academical Institution ('Inst.'), which was founded by his grandfather, and in Liverpool.

He started to practice as a solicitor in 1888, but was sidetracked into arts and culture. He revived the *Ulster Journal of Archaeology* and restored churches and castles, such as Jordan's Castle, Ardglass, Co. Wexford (which he renamed Shane Castle). He also re-erected ancient crosses and gravestones, using his own money to do so. He re-interred HENRY JOY MCCRACKEN's bones in MARY ANN MCCRACKEN's grave in Clifton Street Graveyard.

Bigger was a member of the Royal Irish Academy, and was especially interested in folk music and song. He was elected a Fellow of the Royal Society of Antiquaries of Ireland. In 1894, he edited *Ulster Dialect – Words and Phrases*. He published a number of pamphlets, including *Northern Leaders of '98*, *Irish Penal Crosses* and *The Ulster Land War of 1770*.

Bigger had a private library of 3,000 volumes, which were given to the Belfast Central Library when he died. A selection of his work was published a year after his death as *Articles and Sketches*.

Bigger's home on the Antrim Road, 'Ardrigh', was a regular meeting place for Nationalists, and the block of flats now on the site bears the same name. Bigger died in Belfast on 9th December 1926.

GEORGE A. BIRMINGHAM (JAMES OWEN HANNAY) *(1865–1950)* | Novelist

James Owen Hannay wrote under the *nom de plume* of George A. Birmingham. Born at 75 University Road, Belfast on 16th July 1865, he was educated at Haileybury and Trinity College, Dublin. Hannay entered the Church of Ireland ministry, and became Rector of Westport, Co. Mayo in 1892. He is famed for his statement, 'I was born in Belfast and brought up to believe that like St Paul, I am a citizen of no mean city'.

His first few novels received little attention, but this changed in 1908 when he published *Spanish Gold*, which featured a curate called Meldon. Its humour appealed to the public and he wrote a 'George A. Birmingham' novel almost every year.

His novel *General John Regan* was produced as a play in Westport in 1913. When the local people discovered their Rector was the author, there was a riot and a boycott ensued. Hannay left Westport and served as an army chaplain to the British Embassy in Budapest. He then went to France as army chaplain during the First World War, before settling at Mells Rectory in Somerset in 1924. Later, he took charge of a small parish in London. Besides his novels, Hannay also published some religious works and travel books under his own name, such as *A Padre in France* and biographies of Isaiah and Jeremiah. He published his autobiography in 1934. He died in London on 2nd of February 1950.

DANNY BLANCHFLOWER *(1926–93)* | Footballer

Robert Dennis ('Danny') Blanchflower was one of the most talented footballers of his era. A tactical genius, he captained Tottenham Hotspur to a League and Cup double and a European triumph, captained Northern Ireland to the World Cup Quarter Finals in 1958 and was Footballer of the Year in the same season (he was Footballer of the Year again in 1961).

He was born on February 10th 1926 in Dunraven Park in the Bloomfield area, the son of conscientious, working class parents who ensured he worked hard at Ravenscroft Elementary School. Danny played football for the Boys Brigade and, as a born organiser, set up 'Bloomfield United' on his own – the team played in junior leagues for some years. In 1940 Danny enrolled in a general education course at Belfast Technical College and later gained a scholarship to study on a short course at the University of St Andrews – where he also took up golf.

After the war, in 1945, Blanchflower signed up with Glentoran as a professional, joining Billy Bingham and Jimmy McIlroy at the Oval. After three years at the club, he joined Second Division Barnsley, where he stayed for two seasons before signing for Aston Villa, where he stayed until 1954. In December he joined Tottenham Hotspur, where he orchestrated the midfield. Spurs won the double in 1961, the FA Cup in 1962 and the European Cup Winners' Cup in 1963 – the first UK team to win in Europe.

Northern Ireland's performance in 1958 was in no small part due to Blanchflower's leadership. When his brother Jackie (or 'Twiggy'), born in 1933, was forced to leave football after the Munich Air Disaster, it made Danny even more determined to drive the team on.

In 1964, aged 38, Blanchflower's injuries forced him to quit. Already a columnist, he continued to work for *The Sunday Express*. He also wrote for *The Daily Mail* and *The New Statesman*. Blanchflower managed the Northern Ireland team from 1976 to 1979 and also managed Chelsea for a season, before returning to journalism.

A private man, he was the first person to refuse *This is Your Life* an interview. He could be lively and genial, but on his own terms. Financial hardship was alleviated by a testimonial at White Hart Lane in 1990. By that time, however, Blanchflower was already suffering from Alzheimer's disease. He died in a nursing home in Surrey on 9th December 1993.

Credited with inventing the modern free kick, Blanchflower was an original thinker. The recreation park and sports stadium near Tillysburn in Sydenham, East Belfast was renamed in his honour.

KENNETH BRANAGH *(1960–)* | Actor and Director

Kenneth Charles Branagh was born in the York Street area of Belfast. His father was a joiner and his mother worked in Gallahers Tobacco Factory. Branagh is said to recall life in the area as knockabout and robust but to have enjoyed it.

The family moved to Reading in 1969 to avoid the Troubles. His father started his own business and Kenneth went to school locally. He was accepted for the Royal Academy of Dramatic Art (RADA) in London and was awarded the Bancroft Gold Medal on leaving in 1981. Branagh found work in various projects. Memorably, he acted as Billy in Graham Reid's immensely popular *Billy Plays* trilogy, broadcast on BBC television in the early 1980s. Branagh played alongside JAMES ELLIS, Mark Mulholland and Brid Brennan.

In 1984, Branagh made his mark with the Royal Shakespeare Company for his portrayal of Henry V at Stratford-upon-Avon. He also appeared in television productions like *The Boy in the Bush* (1983) and, with Emma Thompson, the epic *Fortunes of War* (1986–7). Branagh formed his own theatre and film company, Renaissance, and brought his Three Shakespeare Plays tour – *Hamlet*, *As You Like It* and *Much Ado About Nothing* – to Belfast. He directed Shakespeare's *Henry V*, which was voted best film at the Cinema '89 Festival, and was dubbed 'The New Olivier' by the media.

During the 1990s Branagh directed and starred in films such as *Dead Again*, *Much Ado About Nothing*, *Peter's Friends*, *Hamlet*, *In the Bleak Mid-Winter* and *Love's Labours Lost*; his films have all had charity screenings in Belfast in aid of the Northern Ireland Council for Voluntary Action (NICVA) and the Ulster Youth Theatre. He also directed, starred in and co-produced *Mary Shelley's Frankenstein,* with Francis Ford Coppola as Executive Producer, in 1994, and was in Belfast for a premier of the film at the MGM cinema on the Dublin Road.

Branagh's acting and directing output continues to be prodigious.

EDWARD BUNTING *(1773–1843)* | Musician

Edward Bunting was an important figure in the Irish musical movement of the late 18th and 19th centuries. Born in 1773 in Armagh, he went to live in Drogheda with his eldest brother, an organist and music teacher, after his father died.

Bunting made progress under his brother's tuition. Aged 11, he was appointed to the prestigious position of sub-organist in St Anne's Church, Donegall Street, Belfast. He became a popular and successful musician, and also taught, although it is recorded his forthright views on one pupil's talent resulted in Bunting soundly boxing the student's ears!

Bunting's growing interest in Irish traditional music was strongly supported by the McCrackens (see MARY ANN MCCRACKEN), with whom Bunting lodged in High Street. He founded the Belfast Harp Society and the Irish Harp Society, and the 1792 Belfast Harper's Festival inspired Bunting to travel Ireland and collect ancient Irish airs, saving many of them from extinction. The University Press in Dublin published Bunting's *General Collection of the Ancient Music of Ireland* in 1796. It included 76 airs. Another edition was published in 1809, and a third in 1840.

In 1819, Bunting married a Miss Chapman and moved to Dublin. He later became the organist at St Stephen's Church there. Edward Bunting died in 1843 in Dublin aged 70.

MARGARET BYERS *(1832–1912)* | Educationalist

Margaret Byers was a pioneer of women's education in Belfast. She established The Ladies' Collegiate school and lobbied for further education rights for women. She was also a philanthropist and suffragist.

Margaret Byers, pioneering educationalist and founder of Victoria College, Belfast, c.1885

Born Margaret Moore in April 1832 in Rathfriland, she moved to Stoke-on-Trent to live with her uncles when her father, a farmer and flax mill owner, died in 1840. She went to school in Nottingham and then taught at the same school, where a progressive headmistress influenced her thinking on the education of girls.

She married the Reverend John Byers in 1852, but was left a widow with a baby at the age of 21 when her husband died after missionary duty in Shanghai. Adversity only strengthened her resolve, and she returned to teach at the Ladies' Collegiate in Cookstown.

In 1859, Byers opened 'an establishment for the boarding and education of young ladies' at 13 Wellington Place, Belfast. The Ladies' Collegiate started with 35 pupils. It was well-located, as most of the professional middle class still lived in the centre of Belfast.

At this time, there was no proper system of education for girls. Many were taught at home by ill-qualified governesses. Byers succeeded in creating order out of the genteel, haphazard arrangements of the period. The school offered pupils a solid base of learning, including Modern History, Natural Science, basic English Grammar and Arithmetic. Numbers quickly increased, and the school moved to larger premises at 10 Howard Street, and again in the late 1860s to 74–6 Pakenham Place on the Dublin Road. By 1873 the school had to relocate to a site at Lower Crescent which Byers bought from the Corry family, who built Upper and Lower Crescent. She negotiated the moves and handled all the school's finances. The school was to stay at Lower Crescent for almost 100 years. In 1887, Queen Victoria bestowed the title 'Victoria College, Belfast' on the school.

Byers successfully lobbied Government to allow girls to sit exams towards Higher Education. When scholarships were awarded Victoria (as the school was known) was well represented, as it was in the 1890s when past pupils started to attain degree level. Margaret Byers undoubtedly ran an efficient school. Most of her teachers were female, and, by 1874 they were all fully trained. The curriculum increased to include Dancing, Needlework and Cookery. Discipline, apparently, was never a problem.

Byers' dynamism was evident equally in other spheres. She was the first President of the Irish Women's Temperance Union. She also helped organise a Home for Destitute Girls and was a committee member of the Ulster Branch of the National Society for Women's Suffrage. In 1905, she received an honorary degree from Trinity College, Dublin, and in 1908 Queen's University appointed her to its Senate. She died in 1912.

An Ulster History Circle plaque to Byers on the wall of the Crescent Arts Centre in Lower Crescent, commemorates the home of Victoria College from 1873 until 1972.

HUGH McCALMONT CAIRNS (1819–85) | Lord Chancellor of England

Hugh McCalmont Cairns was Lord Chancellor of England from 1868 until he retired in 1880. Disraeli described one of his orations about the Irish Land Bill as 'one of the greatest speeches ever delivered in Parliament'.

Cairns was born in Cultra and educated at Belfast Academy and Trinity College, Dublin, where he graduated with a First in Classics in 1838, followed by a rapid rise to prominence at the London Bar. By 1844, he was one of the Seniors at Lincoln's Inn. In 1856, he was appointed Queen's Counsel and in 1856 he was knighted and became Solicitor General.

Interested in politics, Cairns was elected Member of Parliament for Belfast in 1852. As an MP he became renowned for his logical, rational approach that had been equally responsible for his rise in the legal world. He championed the Protestant church, especially at the time of the Irish Church Bill (became Act in 1869) when the Church of Ireland was disestablished (and Presbyterians also lost the 'regium donum'). He was also involved with the 1879 Irish University Bill and the 1874 Real Property Act.

In 1867, Cairns became Baron Cairns of Garmoyle. He was appointed Lord Chancellor in 1868 and also held the position of Attorney General. In 1878 he was created Earl Cairns and Viscount Garmoyle.

Cairns was married to Mary, and they had five sons and one daughter. Until 1873 they lived in London, and then moved to Bournemouth. He retired in 1880. A close associate of the social reformer, Lord Shaftesbury, he actively supported Barnardo's charity and was a Sunday School teacher. (Incidentally, Lord Shaftesbury's son, Lord Ashby, married into the Chichester family and contributed to the completion of Belfast Castle in 1874. His name is remembered in Shaftesbury Square and Shaftesbury Avenue.) Cairns was regarded as the most prominent lawyer of his time. His logical, rational and at times cold, passionless delivery of an argument both impressed and won the day. He was, however, not renowned for his sense of humour. Quite deaf in his sixties, he spent some of his later years on the Riviera. He died in 1885.

JOSEPH CAMPBELL *(1879–1944)* | Poet

The poet Joseph Campbell (Seosamh Mac Cathmhaoil) was best remembered for the song 'My Lagan Love'. Born in Belfast in 1879, he lived a colourful life.

Campbell was very interested in the Gaelic Cultural Revival. He collaborated with Herbert Hayes in setting words to folk melodies in *Songs of Uladh*, published in 1904 – the collection which includes 'My Lagan Love'. Campbell edited two editions of *Uladh* magazine with Bulmer Hobson and wrote a play entitled *The Little Cowherd of Slainge* for the Ulster Literary Theatre (performed in 1905) before going to live in Dublin.

Later, Campbell settled in London where he became Secretary of the Irish Literary Society, publishing volumes of poetry entitled *The Rushlight* and *The Gilly of Christ*. He made use of Gaelic romantic and rural imagery in his work.

In 1912 he settled in Lackendarragh, Co. Wicklow with his wife Nancy Maude. In the same year, his play *Judgement* was produced at the Abbey Theatre.

Campbell was also interested in politics. He was elected chairman of Wicklow County Council and volunteered his services in the Easter Rising of 1916. He was imprisoned at Mountjoy and then interned at the Curragh for two years as a republican sympathiser.

Campbell lived in the United States between 1923 and 1935. He founded the School of Irish Studies in New York and lectured for ten years in Anglo-Irish literature at Fordham University. In 1939 he returned to Co. Wicklow and lived in seclusion at Glencree farmstead, until his death in 1944. His collected poems were published in 1963.

AMY CARMICHAEL *(1867–1951)* | Missionary

Amy Beatrice Carmichael was born on 16th December 1867 in Millisle, Co. Down, the eldest of seven children. The family was Presbyterian and her father, who died when she was only 18, was a mill owner. She was educated first privately in Harrogate, Yorkshire, and later in Belfast at Victoria College where she had something of a 'tomboy' reputation. She was deeply moved by the poverty of many of those around her in Belfast and embarrassed by her own comfortable status; she became overwhelmed with a sense of needing to help people and act out her faith.

After she left school she immersed herself in philanthropy in Belfast. She founded 'The Welcome' (or Welcome Hall), a centre in Cambrai Street for mill girls of the area, in 1889. After hearing Hudson Taylor of the China Inland Mission (CIM) speaking, she decided to offer herself to Christian missionary work. She was, however, not accepted by CIM, due to physical frailty.

In 1893, Carmichael did become a missionary first going to Japan and then, in 1895, to India, supported by the Keswick Foundation. She worked in Dohnavur, India until her death, founding a rescue mission for 'temple' children, known as the Dohnavur Fellowship. She 'purchased' and brought up young girls who were destined for sale to temples, often for prostitution. Later, she started a home for boys too, and in 1916, she founded The Sisters of the Common Life. One of her notable statements was 'You can give without loving but you cannot love without giving'.

Carmichael published over 35 books, including *Things as They Are* (1903), *Gold Cord* (1932) and the poignant *Rose From Briar* (1933). None of her books carried a photograph, and she is reputed to have said: 'I think nothing can be less beautiful than I am, that there are enough "not" beautiful things in the world without my adding to the number'.

She was dogged by poor health and disabled by a fall in 1931 which by 1949 had fully immobilised her. She died in 1951 and is buried in Dohnavur. On 16th December 1967, a conference was held in 'The Welcome' in Cambrai Street, to mark the centenary of Carmichael's birth.

SIR EDWARD CARSON *(1854–1935)* | Lawyer and Political Leader

One of the most significant figures in the moulding of the Northern Irish State was Sir Edward Henry Carson. Born in Dublin on 9th February 1854, he attended Portarlington School and Trinity College, Dublin. He was called to the Irish Bar in 1877, and quickly built up a substantial practice. Carson was appointed Solicitor General for Ireland in 1892, and was called to the London Bar in 1893. As a lawyer, Carson was probably best known for his rigorous cross-examination of Oscar Wilde in the famous libel action against the Marquess of Queensbury.

By 1900, Unionists were concerned about the Home Rule question. Carson, who was MP for Trinity College, joined the Unionist Government in 1900 as Solicitor General. In Parliament he opposed any weakening of the Union, and in 1910 became leader of the Unionists. When the Liberals introduced the Home Rule Bill in 1912, Ulster Unionists stiffened their opposition. Carson took a leading part in forming the Ulster Volunteers in 1913. Thousands signed the Solemn Covenant of Resistance to Home Rule (some in their own blood) at Belfast City Hall, backed by Carson – the first to sign – who stated, 'Don't be afraid of illegalities'.

The Home Rule Bill got Royal Assent in August 1914, but the First World War intervened and the Bill was suspended. In 1915, Carson was appointed Attorney General, holding the position for a year. Later, he accepted the position of First Lord of the Admiralty. Carson became MP for Duncairn after World War I. His original intention was to maintain the Union for all Ireland, whereas JAMES CRAIG wanted to maintain the union in order to save 'Protestant Ulster'. After much negotiation it was agreed that six counties of the Province of Ulster would become Northern Ireland on 1 May 1921, under the 1920 Better Government of Ireland Act. The State Opening of Parliament by King George V was held in Belfast City Hall on 22nd June 1921. Union Theological College on Botanic Avenue was used as the Parliament's venue until the Parliament Buildings at Stormont were opened by the Prince of Wales in November 1932. In 1921 Carson relinquished his joint partnership to Craig, who became Northern Ireland's first Prime Minister. Carson was appointed Lord of Appeal and became a life peer as Baron Carson of Duncairn. To mark his influence on the creation of the Northern Ireland state, a massive bronze statue of Carson was erected in front of Stormont in 1932 – Carson unveiled it himself on his last visit to Northern Ireland.

Carson died in Kent on 22nd October 1935. After a state funeral in Belfast, he was buried in St Anne's Cathedral, where a bronze memorial plaque – by the renowned

Holywood sculptor Rosamund Praeger – marks the spot in the south aisle. He is the only person, so far, to be buried in the Cathedral.

FRANK CARSON *(1926–)* | Comedian

Frank Carson is renowned for his catchphrase 'It's the way I tell 'em!' and his infectious laugh. Now internationally recognised for his natural comic talent, he was born and grew up in a tenement house in Great Patrick Street, in the Sailortown area of Belfast. He is one of five children.

Carson attended St Patrick's School on Donegall Street, and was a boy soprano in the church choir. He left school at 14. He worked in a Smithfield booksellers on Saturdays from the age of twelve, earning half a crown, two shillings of which he gave to his mother. Carson became a plasterer, and his skills are in evidence in Maysfield Presbyterian Church and the grotto next to St Mary's Church in Chapel Lane. He also served for a time as a member of the Parachute Regiment.

With dreams of one day being famous, he joined a minstrel troupe at Belfast Newsboys Club in York Street – a cross-community venture. He often went by the nickname 'Snowball'. Gigs in community halls led to the well-known Ulster Television newsreader Ivor Mills giving Carson a slot on his variety programme on UTV. Since the 1960s his comic act has taken him to English clubs and subsequently all around the world; he has given command perform-ances at the London Palladium.

Carson has been married to his wife Ruth for over 50 years, and they have three children. They have homes in both Blackpool and Balbriggan, Co. Dublin; Carson has been Mayor of Balbriggan twice. Once asked if there was anything he was serious about, he described his sense of pride in being a Papal Knight of St Gregory, which is the highest honour the Roman Catholic Church can bestow. He was presented with the accolade at an audience with Pope John Paul II on March 28, 1988 after Bishop Edward Daly in Derry, amongst others, informed the Vatican of his tireless charity work.

SIR ARTHUR CHICHESTER *(1563–1625)* | Lord Deputy of Ireland

Sir Arthur Chichester effectively founded Belfast in 1603 when a Royal Charter granted him Belfast Castle (then near present-day High Street). Later, as Lord Chichester of Belfast, he helped mastermind the Plantation of Ulster and organised the first Irish Parliament for 27 years. The Chichester dynasty was to rule Belfast until 1840 when local government was reformed and councillors were elected. The origin of the Chichesters' Donegall title comes from the time when Sir Arthur Chichester was granted the lands of the O'Dohertys in Inishowen, Co. Donegal in the early 17th century.

Born in England in 1563, Chichester captained one of Drake's ships to the West Indies, but it was his services to the Crown in Ireland that won royal approval. He set about the task of subduing the Chief of Clandeboye's forces with a will. In 1595 Chichester was knighted for his services and in 1599 he was appointed Governor of Carrickfergus, which had been an established port for centuries. Partly due to Chichester's efforts, Belfast was to become the more significant port.

On 5th November 1603, Chichester, for his services to the Crown, was given 'The Castle of Belfaste, with the appurtenants and hereditaments situate in the Lower Clandeboye.' Now in control of the area, Chichester set about rebuilding Belfast Castle. Under his guidance, the Town started to flourish. He sublet lands adjoining the Castle. In 1605, he was appointed Lord Deputy – he was the longest serving one, from 1605 to 1616 – and was responsible for all Ireland. In 1603, he drafted his own scheme for Plantation by

Portrait of Sir Arthur Chichester, Baron of Belfast, (artist unknown, 19th century), Belfast Harbour Office

Scottish settlers, who started to arrive in 1606.

In 1612, Chichester was created Baron Chichester of Belfast, and in 1613 the Town received a charter proclaiming it as a Corporate Borough. The King had political reasons for this. He wanted to call a Parliament and was keen to ensure a Protestant majority; hence the creation of new boroughs which were all entitled to return two members – Belfast was one of 40 new boroughs created throughout Ireland. Chichester, as Lord of the Castle, was able to appoint the two Members of Parliament. In 1613, he was also appointed Lord Baron of Belfast, and had complete control of Belfast and its political life with the power to appoint a Sovereign (today's Lord Mayor) and twelve burgesses.

Chichester left Ireland in 1622 and died in London three years later. He is buried in St Nicholas' Church in Carrickfergus where a fine monument was erected to his memory. The Chichesters lived in Belfast until 1708, when the Old Castle on a site around present-day Castle Lane burned down. The family then left for England and became absentee land-lords. In 1802 the Second Marquess of Donegall, George Augustus, returned to Belfast and lived at Donegall Place before building a new house at Ormeau in 1824. The family left the house in the 1860s, and moved to the new Belfast Castle (designed by Lanyon, Lynn and Lanyon – see SIR CHARLES LANYON) on the slopes of Cavehill in 1870.

SIR GEORGE CLARK *(1860–1935)* | Shipbuilder

Born in Paisley, Scotland, George Smith Clark was a partner in shipbuilding concern Workman Clark and Co. Clark's family had been involved for some generations in the Scottish textile industry. George Clark and his partner Frank Workman both served their time as appren-tices at Harland & Wolff (see EDWARD HARLAND and GUSTAV WOLFF). They stayed on long enough to reach junior management, then set up on their own in 1880 on the Co. Antrim bank of the River Lagan.

A steam coaster by the name of *Ethel* was the first product of the 'wee yard', as it came to be called. By 1891, Workman Clark and Co. had moved to a large fourteen-acre site and set up an engineering works. Maintaining a foundry on the Clyde, Workman Clark moved into the niche area of specialist ships and thrived. They built fruit carriers and pioneered refrigerated ships that brought cheap lamb from New Zealand.

By 1900, 'the wee yard' had two engineering works and ten building berths. Inevitably, it would always be overshadowed by Harland & Wolff, but it was the sixth largest UK yard, with a worldwide reputation, and in 1902 its 750,000 ton output was the greatest of any UK yard. Workman Clark survived the First World War and the troubles of the early 1920s, but the worldwide depression of the 1930s was too much for it and in 1935 it closed. The last ship to be delivered was a tanker, *Acarus*. It was the 536th vessel to come out of the yard.

As well as running the shipyard, Clark was also a member of the Northern Ireland Senate (then the upper house of the Parliament at Stormont) from 1925 to 1935, and was its Deputy Speaker from 1932 to 1934, for which he was knighted.

JOHN COLE *(1927–)* | Journalist

A political commentator and experienced newsman with an instantly recognisable voice, John Cole was an important media figure for many years. Born in Belfast on 23rd November 1927, he attended Fortwilliam and Skegoneil primary schools and later Belfast Royal Academy. He graduated externally from London University.

Cole started his career in 1945 at the *Belfast Telegraph*, first as a reporter and then as its political correspondent. In 1956 he joined *The Guardian* in Manchester, working first as labour correspondent, before becoming News Editor, and later Deputy Editor.

Cole joined *The Observer* in 1975 and worked as Deputy Editor of the paper for six years. In 1981, he joined the BBC as its political editor and his distinctive voice soon became very familiar. Known to be modest and self-effacing, he was also renowned for his tenacity in

following a story. His distinguished journalistic skills led to awards from the Royal Television Society and BAFTA. He has several honorary degrees.

Cole also wrote political columns for *The Listener* and the *New Statesman*, and has written several books: *The Poor of the Earth* about Third-World employment, *The Thatcher Years*, political memoirs entitled *As It Seemed to Me,* and a novel, *A Clouded Peace.* He 'retired' in October 1992, and lives with his wife Madge in Surrey. They have four sons.

WILLIAM CONOR *(1881–1968)* | Artist

For those with even a passing interest in Northern Irish/Irish art, William Conor's work will be familiar. His are the pictures and sketches of shipyard workers, mill girls and 'shawlies', children playing in the street.

Born in Fortingale Street in the Old Lodge Road district, Conor studied at the Belfast School of Art and went on to become a Lithographic Technician in the Poster Design Department of David Allen and Sons. He left after several years, deciding to concentrate on painting, and within a few years he was an exhibiting member of the Belfast Art Society. He was appointed the official War Artist during the First World War and spent his time visiting munitions works and army camps.

After the end of the First World War, he went to London. Despite befriending painters Augustus John and SIR JOHN LAVERY, and having four pictures accepted for the London National Portrait Society exhibition, Conor was never really happy in London and was glad to return to Belfast to paint *The Opening of the First Northern Ireland Parliament in 1921*– held in Belfast City Hall on 22nd June 1921. Further exhibitions followed in Belfast, Dublin and London, where the famous painting *The Launch* was displayed. He was appointed War Artist again in 1939, and participated in several exhibitions at the Council for the Encouragement of Music and Art (CEMA) in the 1940s.

Conor was awarded an O.B.E. in 1952, and was appointed President of the Royal Ulster Academy in 1957. However, he often felt unfulfilled and isolated. Despite friendships with writers like JOSEPH TOMELTY and Lynn Doyle, he remained, despite his achievements, a shy man – he lived modestly without achieving real financial success.

Working from home, Conor remained active into his eighties, with exhibitions at the Bell Gallery and the Arts Club. He died at his home in Salisbury Avenue, aged 87, leaving much of his work to the Linen Hall Library. After his death the Arts Council held the first of many retrospective exhibitions.

Conor is remembered as a painter who felt at home with his subject matter of the Belfast streets. The mood of his work was always genial, with a spiritual abundance that captured Belfast life brilliantly. His former studio (now a café bearing his name) is at 11a Stranmillis Road.

CARDINAL WILLIAM CONWAY *(1913–77)* | Roman Catholic Archbishop of Armagh and Primate of All Ireland

Born in now-demolished Dover Street, William Conway attended Boundary Street Primary School, Barrack Street Christian Brothers School and Queen's University Belfast. He went on to attend Maynooth Seminary and was ordained a priest in 1937; he was made Doctor of Divinity the following year.

After studying Canon Law at the Gregorian University, Rome from 1938 to 1941, Conway returned to Belfast and taught English and Latin at St Malachy's College, Belfast from 1941 to 1942. He then returned to Maynooth to take up the position of Professor of Moral

Cardinal William Conway, Catholic Archbishop of Armagh, founder of Trócaire

Theology and became Professor of Canon Law in 1943. He held both chairs until 1958, when he was ordained Bishop.

He administrated at St Mary's Parish Dundalk in 1958, also working as Editor of the *Irish Theological Quarterly*. On 10th September 1963, William Conway was appointed Archbishop of Armagh and Primate of All Ireland and on 22nd February 1965 was created a Cardinal.

Cardinal Conway often attended Vatican Council meetings in Rome and was a member of four Vatican Congregations, including Education. He spoke often at the Second Vatican Council. Conway was also involved in the reform of Canon Law as a member of the Pontifical Committee.

Cardinal Conway is possibly best known for setting up Trócaire, the Catholic agency for development aid.

Cardinal Conway died in Armagh on 17th April 1977.

HENRY COOKE *(1788–1868)* | Presbyterian Moderator and Polemicist

Doctor Henry Cooke's statue stands in College Square East, as large as he once was in Belfast life. This founding father of Presbyterian fundamentalism came to prominence at a point when life in the city started to change dramatically. Born in Grillagh near Maghera on 11th May 1788, Cooke was educated locally and at the University of Glasgow. In 1808 he was ordained into the Presbyterian ministry and was given a church in Duneane, near Randalstown.

In 1815, he resumed his studies at Glasgow University and attended the Royal College of Surgeons in Dublin in 1817. The following year Cooke returned north as pastor of Killyleagh. Cooke came to the fore in the 1820s. In 1824 he was appointed Moderator of the Synod of Ulster and in both 1841 and 1862, he was Moderator of the General Assembly. Cooke campaigned strongly against Catholic emancipation and in 1827 drove the radical and liberal Presbyterians from the Synod. On a personal level, Cooke was on friendly terms with BARNEY HUGHES, a Catholic businessman, and performed his wedding ceremony (to a Presbyterian).

Support for Cooke grew, accentuated somewhat by Protestant fears over the large Catholic rural influx due to the Industrial Revolution. In 1829, his supporters built May Street Presbyterian Church. When the New Board of National Education was established, Cooke perceived a threat to Protestant education. Under his guidance, the Synod organised its own scheme and secured recognition in 1840 from the Board.

When Daniel O'Connell, the charismatic leader of the Catholic emancipation movement, came to Belfast in January 1841, Cooke organised a rally to counter his rival,

Statue of Henry Cooke, outside Inst. in College Square East, photographed before the building of Belfast Technical College

which resulted in riots.

Cooke secured a government grant for the Union Theological College in Belfast (designed by SIR CHARLES LANYON), and was later appointed President and Dean in Residence in 1849. He was Professor of Rhetoric in the Theological College of the General Assembly in 1855, and was instrumental in establishing the Free Church of Scotland.

Cooke's energy was phenomenal. He rose at 4 a.m. to write pamphlets, sermons and magazine articles. He also edited a new version of *Brown's Family Bible.*

Cooke died aged 80 at his house on the Ormeau Road on 13th December 1868. He was married to Ellen Mann of Toomebridge and they had 13 children. He is buried in Balmoral Cemetery.

Contrary to popular belief, Cooke's statue of 1876 by S.F. Lynn was not placed with its back to Inst. as a sleight to the College (although he was no friend to the establishment) – the statue of Frederick Richard, Earl of Belfast by PATRICK MCDOWELL, which it replaced, also had its back to the building.

SIR JAMES CRAIG (1871–1940) | First Prime Minister of Northern Ireland

James Craig was born in Belfast into a wealthy family. He was educated in Edinburgh and worked for the family stockbroking firm in Belfast before joining the Royal Irish Rifles in the South African War of 1899–1902.

In 1906 he was elected MP for East Down, a constituency he represented until 1918, when he transferred to Mid Down. Craig became increasingly involved in politics as the Home Rule issue loomed large prior to the First World War. He was instrumental in organising the Ulster Volunteer Force, and strongly supported EDWARD CARSON in his anti-Home Rule lobby. Craig was also the Ulster representative at Buckingham Palace in 1914 at the time of the third Home Rule Bill, when the number of Ulster counties to be left out of Home Rule was discussed but not agreed to.

During the First World War, Craig was Quarter Master General in France in the 36th Division. After the war, in 1918, he received a knighthood and took on the role of Parliamentary Secretary in Lloyd George's government. In 1920 he was appointed First Lord of the Admiralty.

Craig participated in the drafting of the Government of Ireland Act, which led to the establishment of Northern Ireland. When Carson gave up the leadership of the Ulster Unionists, Craig became Prime Minister in 1921, and he retained the position until his death. He was already MP for North Down. He was created Viscount Craigavon in 1927.

Under Craig, the Unionists established complete dominance in local politics. Craig abolished Proportional Representation in 1921, bolstering the Unionist position. The May 1921 election saw the party capture 40 out of 52 seats; the remaining seats were 6 Nationalist and 6 Sinn Féin. This trend did not alter over the next 19 years while he was Prime Minister. Craig was responsible for the United Kingdom's first devolved government in what he saw as 'a Protestant state'.

When Craig died peacefully in his armchair on 24th November 1940, just after listening to the 6 o'clock news, he was replaced by his deputy, John Andrews (elder brother of the *Titanic*'s designer, Thomas Andrews) as Prime Minister. He was buried at Stormont. Craig's grand house, 'Craigavon', on Circular Road in East Belfast was used by the UVF for training. It later became the UVF Hospital caring for 36th Ulster Division soldiers injured in the First World War.

JAMES CROMBIE (1730–90) | Educationalist and Presbyterian Minister

The Reverend Doctor James Crombie had the distinction of both founding Belfast Academy (later Belfast Royal Academy), reputedly the oldest school in Belfast, and being Minister of First Presbyterian Church, Rosemary Street, the oldest surviving place of worship in the city.

Crombie was born in Perth, Scotland, on 16th December 1730. He matriculated at the University of St Andrews in 1748, and was licensed at Strathbogie Presbytery in 1757 where he became parish schoolmaster. Crombie was ordained at Elgin on 11th September 1760. He became tutor to the Earl of Moray's family, and then returned to his studies in Glasgow.

In 1769, Crombie was offered a stipend of £80 a year and £10 for a house to accept a position at Belfast's First Presbyterian Church. He agreed, and for a number of years worked alongside James Mackay. When Mackay died in 1781, Crombie became sole pastor. A dynamic man who delivered his sermons with enthusiasm, he soon increased the congregation. In 1783, the larger congregation was housed in a new meeting house in Rosemary Street.

In 1774, Crombie married Elizabeth Simpson – they were to have four sons and one daughter. In 1783, Crombie was awarded a doctorate in Divinity from St Andrews. He was renowned for his liberal views, tolerance and energy. In the late 1780s, he was in favour of

Sunday drill for volunteers. He was a member of First Belfast Volunteers and sometimes preached on Sundays in his uniform.

Always interested in education, Crombie decided to establish a school in Belfast. On 9th September 1785, an ambitious prospectus was issued for Belfast Academy. Funds were subscribed, and the Academy opened with Crombie as Principal. He also taught Classics, Philosophy and History. The Academy was opened at 2 Academy Street (near St Anne's Cathedral today) on a 99-year lease from Lord Donegall. It moved to Cliftonville Road in 1878.

Crombie's labours led to a decline in his health. Nevertheless, he worked on until his death in 1790.

FRED DALY *(1911–89)* | Golfer

A familiar face around South Belfast for many years, Fred Daly remains the only golfer from Ireland to win the British Open Championship. Born in Portrush, Daly started as a caddy for a shilling a round. When he wasn't carrying clubs, he was playing and at 17 he gave up a job as an electrician to become a golf professional at Mahee.

Daly rose through good performances in the Ulster and Irish Championships which led to a place on the Irish team. When he travelled he often had to rely on a local steward finding him digs, and often a berth on the ferry was beyond his means.

He played more and more events in the UK, building up experience, and won the Irish Open in 1946. In 1947 he became professional at the prestigious Balmoral course in South Belfast, after spells in Lurgan and Londonderry. 1947 also saw Daly's greatest triumph, when he won the Open at Hoylake, seeing off the close challenge of American Frank Stranahan. Daly completed the four rounds in 193, which was a high-figures score but largely due to continual rain. His win earned him the princely sum of £150.

By all accounts, the party sparked off by his victory on the boat back to Belfast was memorable – Daly always admitted he loved life as much as golf. He didn't practice for hours on end, preferring to help inexperienced golfers, or unwind after a round.

Daly came third in the 1950 Open, and just lost out to Bobby Locke in 1951. He won the British Professional Matchplay title in 1947, 1949 and 1953. He won the Irish Open three times, the Ulster Open eight times, and was selected for the Ryder Cup team four times in the 1940s and 1950s. He was Balmoral professional until 1974. In 1980, the 'Daly Corner' was erected in the clubhouse, with a permanent display of his achievements. He only gave up the game in the mid-1980s, and his son Robin succeeded him as club professional. In 1984 he was accepted into the Texaco Hall of Fame.

In 1983, Fred Daly was awarded an MBE. On 18th November that year he died suddenly of a heart attack at his home in Bawnmore Road. He was 79 and was survived by his wife and two sons.

SIR SAMUEL DAVIDSON *(1846–1921)* | Inventor and Founder of Sirocco Works

Samuel C. Davidson was responsible for Sirocco Works, a Belfast business that made world-wide impact, producing a host of industrial inventions. Born in 1846, he lived at the family home, 'Turf Lodge' in Sydenham, East Belfast. He left school at 15 and was interested in photography and had a dark room at home. He worked in a surveyor's office and then went to India at his cousin James's invitation, to a tea estate in which his father had a share.

Davidson showed promise and soon became a manager. After his father died in 1869, Samuel became a co-partner in the tea estate. It wasn't long before he turned his talents and attention to improving tea drying techniques. His tea drier was perfected and patented in 1877. A friend was astonished by the volume of hot air produced by the machine and likened it to the Sirocco wind. Davidson decided to use 'Sirocco' as a catch-all name for all his products. Selling the tea estate, he patented 120 inventions and the fans were used in every conceivable place, including battleships, coal mines and submarines. His company Samuel Davidson & Co – later Sirocco Works – was established in the Short Strand area of the city in 1881. Notably, the company built the first air conditioning system in the world for the Royal Victoria Hospital in Belfast.

Davidson also helped organise associated Sirocco businesses globally, covering many industrial needs. During the Second World War, Sirocco made ventilators for munitions stores. The business continued to flourish, although it went through changes in later years. In the late 1980s it was taken over by the Scottish engineering group, Howden. Initially this proved successful with new boiler contracts worldwide. In 1987, Charter took the company over. The works closed in 2000.

Among the many inventions for which Davidson is remembered is the peat briquette. He received his K.B.E. in 1921 and died before the year was out. He is buried in the City Cemetery on the Falls Road.

JOSEPH DEVLIN *(1871–1934)* | Nationalist Politician

In the early era of Unionist domination at Stormont, Joe Devlin was one of few influential Nationalists. He used his debating skills to argue the Nationalist case forcefully, while retaining the respect of his Unionist colleagues.

Devlin was born on 13th of February 1871, at Hamill Street, Belfast. Educated at the Christian Brothers School in Divis Street, he worked in a pub for a time, then as a journalist for the *Irish News* and later as Belfast correspondent for the *Freeman's Journal*.

In 1886, he assisted with Thomas Sexton's successful Nationalist campaign in West Belfast. He became Secretary of the Belfast Young Ireland Society before working for the United Irish League in Dublin. In 1902 Devlin stood unopposed in North Kilkenny and entered Westminster, before successfully contesting the West Belfast seat in 1906 and winning it from the Unionists by the narrowest of margins. He held the seat until 1918. His success was partly due to his astute re-founding of the Ancient Order of Hibernians as a political rival to the Orange Order.

He encouraged Catholic Nationalists to join the British Army in the First World War, believing that Home Rule would follow after the War. Recruiting offices were set up on the Falls Road in October 1914. He addressed a meeting of the Irish National Volunteers at the Clonard Picture House on the Falls Road and encouraged them to join the Irish Brigade which was to be an amalgamation of the 10th and 16th Irish Divisions of the British Army. Although Asquith supported the idea they remained separate divisions. Both the 36th (Ulster) and 16th Divisions distinguished themselves at the Somme but suffered heavy losses. Of nearly 11,000 men in the 16th Division, an estimated 4,500 were killed or wounded. When the Belfast survivors of the 16th Division returned to Belfast in 1919 they were welcomed home at Celtic Park (now the site of the Park Centre) by Devlin and other leading Nationalists.

Opposed to partition, Devlin nevertheless took his seat in the Northern Ireland Parliament, first for West Belfast and then for Belfast Central, but was often frustrated by Unionist policies. He was also MP for Fermanagh and Tyrone at Westminster from 1929.

Devlin campaigned for better public housing and better Catholic education. He died, unmarried, on 18th February 1934. Hugely popular with his constituents and known as 'Wee Joe', he was mourned by Nationalists and Unionists alike at his funeral.

GERARD DILLON *(1916–71)* | Artist

Gerard Dillon was a Belfast-born artist whose striking, almost primitive style endeared his work to collectors and buyers worldwide. Born at 26 Lower Clonard Street, off the Falls Road, Dillon was the youngest of eight children. His father Joseph was a postman. Dillon attended Raglan Street School and the Christian Brothers, but left school at 14 to become a house-painter. His mother enrolled him at the Belfast College of Art, but he left after three months.

Aged 18, Dillon went to London where he stayed until 1939, and earned a living with various odd jobs. In 1936, and practically self-taught, he started to paint seriously, going to Connemara to draw inspiration for his landscapes.

In 1942, Dillon presented his first one-man show at the Country Shop, Dublin. In 1943 he exhibited for the first time in the Irish Exhibition of Living Art, where he later displayed regularly. Dillon and his friends Dan O'Neill and George Campbell exhibited wherever they could.

Dillon lived mostly in London between 1945 and 1968, but his work often took him elsewhere. He enjoyed the freedom and obscurity of living in London. The Council for the Encouragement of Music and the Arts (CEMA) put on one-man shows of his work in 1946 and 1950. His work was also exhibited at the Guggenheim International in New York and the Marzotto Exhibition in Rome.

Dillon moved to Dublin in 1968 and lectured there for two years. His *Black Lake* was reproduced as a postage stamp. He also displayed at the Dawson Gallery and designed sets and costumes for the Abbey Theatre. He died in Adelaide Hospital on 14th June 1971. His paintings are on display in many collections in Ireland, including that of the Ulster Museum.

BISHOP PATRICK DORRIAN *(1814–85)* | Bishop of Down and Connor, School and Hospital Founder

Patrick Dorrian, Bishop of Down and Connor, was an important figure in both the fields of religion and education in the 19th century. He was born on 29th March 1814 in Downpatrick. Educated at Maynooth, he was ordained in 1837, and was Curate of Belfast until 1847. He was Parish Priest at Loughinisland from 1847 until 1860.

In 1860, he became Bishop of Gabala, Syria, and five years later became Bishop of Down and Connor. He was energetic, and made many changes in church procedure, totally revolutionising the parish system. In Belfast he dissolved the Holywood/Ballymacarett parish in 1866, creating a separate parish in Holywood and arranging Ballymacarrett as part of the mensal parish of Belfast.

Dorrian organised funds to improve church accommodation and established schools throughout Belfast, including St Patrick's in Donegall Street and St Malachy's in Oxford Street. He also bequeathed his library to the Diocesan College.

Dorrian wrestled with the Belfast Corporation over the new cemetery at Milltown. The Church was offered what is now Falls Park as a Catholic burial place and it was to be part of the City Cemetery, with an underground wall separating the Protestant and Catholic burial grounds. Eventually, a compromise was reached, whereby Dorrian purchased 15 acres at Milltown and consecrated it as a cemetery in 1870. Furthermore, he established an industrial school for boys at Milltown, and was instrumental in St Patrick's female orphanage being certified as an industrial school for girls. He also appointed a priest as an ecclesiastical inspector to examine schools in the Belfast area.

During the 1870s, Dorrian arranged for the Sisters of Nazareth and Clonard Lodge to be established as convents. He was also responsible for what started as Bedeque House on the Crumlin Road in 1883. Run by the Sisters of Mercy, it later became the Mater Hospital.

Dorrian also replaced the 1815 St Patrick's Church in Donegall Street with the present impressive Victorian Gothic building which was opened in August 1877.

Dorrian's only slight failure was his foundation of the newspaper *The Ulster Examiner* – the attitudes of the journalists he employed were considered less than suitable, and the project failed.

Dorrian died on 3rd November 1885 in Belfast. His remains lie in St Patrick's Church.

BARRY DOUGLAS *(1960–)* | Classical Musician

Barry Douglas has built a reputation as an international musician of outstanding talent. Born in Belfast in 1960, he was educated at Methodist College, Belfast (Methody) and also studied at the Belfast School of Music on Donegall Pass.

Barry Douglas

Although an accomplished player of clarinet, 'cello and organ, he decided to concentrate on the piano and won the local heat of the Young Musician of the Year, coming third in the national competition. In 1980 he made his professional debut with the Ulster Orchestra and started a four-year course at the Royal College of Music in London. He then studied with Maria Curcio (a pupil of Arthur Schnabel), Yvegeny Malinin – a professor at the Moscow Conservatoire, and with Alfred Brendel in London. He studied conducting with Jerzy Semkov (Mavrinsky's assistant with the St Petersburg Philharmonic – then Leningrad Philharmonic) and with Marek Janowski, music director of the Dresden Philarmonic Orchestra.

In May 1982 he won the Carnegie Hall Recital award. Over the next few years, Douglas played regular concerts throughout the UK and Europe, but his major international breakthrough came when he won the Tchaikovsky International Piano Competition in Moscow in July 1986. Douglas was the first westerner since Van Cliburn in 1958 to win the coveted prize outright, and the effect on his career was dramatic. He started working with the world's major orchestras including the Berlin Philharmonic and Leipzig Gewandhaus. (After winning in Moscow he played two concerts on consecutive nights at the Ulster Hall – tickets were in such demand that some fans sent blank cheques in order to get seats.) Douglas has since performed regularly in Ireland with both the Ulster Orchestra and the National Symphony Orchestra.

Douglas's success has continued and – apart from taking a year off in 1992/3 to study at Oxford and learn a new repertoire – he has travelled all over the world. He also founded the highly successful Camerata Ireland chamber orchestra in 1999. Made up of musicians from both Northern Ireland and the Republic, it has toured in North and South America and has invitations to play all over the world.

Now based in Paris, he is married to Lurgan-born Deirdre. They have three children, Saoirse, Fergus and Liam. Douglas is revered and welcomed in his home city and his portrait by Tom Philips hangs in the Ulster Museum. He received an honorary doctorate in Music from Queen's in 1987 and an honorary Fellowship of the Royal College of Music, where he is also Prince Consort Professor of Piano. He was awarded the O.B.E. in 2002.

WILLIAM DRENNAN *(1754–1820)* | Political Figure and Educationalist

Born in Belfast on 23rd May 1754 at the manse of First Presbyterian Church, Rosemary Street where his father was minister, William Drennan studied Medicine in Glasgow and Edinburgh and qualified as a doctor. He practised briefly as a gynaecologist in Belfast before going to work in Newry. He is acknowledged as one of the pioneers of inoculation against smallpox, and for promoting hand washing to prevent the spread of disease.

In 1789 Drennan went to Dublin. A man of nationalistic beliefs, he was the originator of the United Irishmen and wrote many political and religious pamphlets. In 1794 he was tried for sedition on 10 counts. Acquitted, he withdrew from the United Irishmen but remained committed to radical politics and was particularly interested in Catholic emancipation. In 1800 he married a wealthy Englishwoman, Sarah Swanwick, gave up Medicine and returned to Belfast to live at Cabin Hill (now the site of Campbell College's Preparatory School). In 1807, determined education should be non-denominational, he founded the Belfast Academical Institution ('Inst.') in College Square East in collaboration with John Templeton and John Hancock. (Inst. became the Royal Belfast Academical Institution in the 1830s.)

Drennan was also interested in literature. He was the founder and editor of *The Belfast Magazine* for several years. In 1795 he coined the phrase 'The Emerald Isle' in the verse 'When Erin First Rose'. In 1814 he blended satire, comment and translations in *Fugitive Verses*. In many ways, he was the only writer of his era to have stood the test of time.

Drennan died on 5th February 1820. He had requested that his coffin pass by Inst.'s grounds. 'Let six poor Protestants and six poor Catholics get a guinea piece for carriage of me, and a priest and a dissenting clergyman with any friends that chuse.' His cortege stopped for a few minutes at the gate of the new college on its way to Clifton Street Graveyard.

Drennan had four sons and a daughter. One of his sons, Dr John Swanwick Drennan, carried on the family medical and literary tradition. His poetry was posthumously published in *Poems and Sonnets*. A liberal Unionist, his writings reflected anti-Home Rule sentiment, eschewing the nationalistic beliefs of his father. John Swanwick Drennan lived in Belfast from 1809 until 1893.

RITA DUFFY *(1959–)* | Artist

Born in Belfast in 1959, the artist Rita Duffy has established herself locally and internationally since the late 1980s.

She took a course in Foundation Studies at Ulster Polytechnic in 1978–9 and followed this with an honours degree in Art and Design in Belfast. Between 1985 and 1986, Duffy studied for an MA in Fine Art at the University of Ulster.

She has been part of Worldwide Collective exhibitions. Her individual shows have been displayed at the Arts Council Gallery, the Ormeau Baths Gallery, the Hugh Lane Gallery in Dublin, the Museum of Contemporary Art, Zagreb and numerous galleries in the United States. Her style originally drew heavily on the local situation, and over the past two decades she has established herself as a figurative/narrative artist

Rita Duffy

concerned with socio-political aspects of life in Northern Ireland. Recently, her work has shown occasional glimpses of humour and fantasy, although most of her symbolism still leans towards the present situation.

In 2001, her project 'Drawing the Blinds' formed part of the Belfast Festival at Queen's – a giant illuminated tapestry of images was attached to the window as blinds on the south-facing façade of the Divis Flats towerblock on Divis Street. The project was inspired by GERARD DILLON who used to create images on his window blinds and switch them on at night to entertain children. The image of Divis Flats has often been used in Duffy's work because, she has said, they 'represent for me the tenacity of this unique city'.

JOHN BOYD DUNLOP *(1840–1921)* | Inventor of the Pneumatic Tyre

John Boyd Dunlop invented the first pneumatic tyre whilst living in Belfast and working as a veterinary surgeon. Born in Ayrshire in 1840, Dunlop was educated at Irvine Academy. He qualified as a vet in 1859, and moved to Belfast in 1867.

He set up his practice at 50 Gloucester Street off May Street. When his son Johnny was prescribed some cycling to counter a heavy cold, Dunlop set about experimenting with his son's tricycle. Dunlop used the idea of air between the wheel and the ground. He developed this by fitting inflated tubes covered in canvas jackets to hoops. Rubber solution bonded it together, and on 28th February 1888, his son's trial run proved a success.

John Boyd Dunlop, inventor of the pneumatic tyre

Dunlop secured his invention as patent number 10607 of 1888. Although he hadn't invented the tyre as such, he was the first person to apply the word 'pneumatic'. He approached W. Edlin and Co. and asked them to make frames that would fit the Dunlop tyres. At first the public was
sceptical, but things changed when Willie Hume, Captain of the Belfast Cruiser Cycle Club, won a race at Cherryvale on 18th May 1889, using Dunlop tyres.

Paper manfacturer Harvey du Cros was in the crowd at Cherryvale. Seven years later, he bought Dunlop's patents and businesses for three million pounds. In 1892, John Dunlop moved to Blackrock, Dublin, and linked up with Bowden and Gillies, who designed frames and could cope with the increased demand. Dunlop was a director. Dunlop spent the rest of his life in Dublin. He died of a slight chill aged 81 on 24th October 1921. His innovation is still important today.

There is plenty of evidence of Dunlop's early work. Two early Edlin pneumatic safety cycles are on display in the Ulster Museum. The Ulster Folk and Transport Museum is home to some early cycles with Dunlop tyres, and the first experimental tyre presented by Dunlop is still on display in the Royal Museum of Scotland. In August 1990, the Northern Bank issued £10 notes, featuring Dunlop.

ARCHBISHOP ROBIN EAMES *(1937–)* | Church of Ireland Archbishop of Armagh, Primate of All Ireland

Robert (Robin) Henry Alexander Eames was born on 27th April 1937 and raised in a Methodist Manse. He was educated at both Belfast Royal Academy and Methodist College, Belfast, before going on to study Law at Queen's University, where he also took a doctorate.

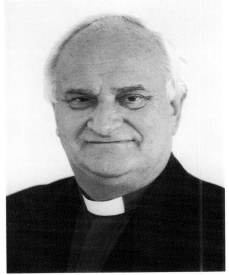

After ordination into the Church of Ireland, Eames served as a curate in Bangor from 1963 until he was appointed Rector of St Dorothea's, Gilnahirk in 1966. In 1974 he went to St Mark's, Dundela as Rector.

In 1975 Eames was elected Bishop of Derry and Raphoe. In 1980, he returned to live in Belfast when he became Bishop of Down and Dromore. In March 1986, he was elected Archbishop of Armagh and Primate of All Ireland, and from the outset he was known for his concilia-tory and leadership skills both in Ireland and the Anglican Communion (indeed, in 1990 there was press spec-ulation that he was being considered for Archbishop of Canterbury). Chair of the Commission on Communion and Women in the Episcopate in 1988–9, he was the first Archbishop of Armagh to see the ordination of

Archbishop Robin Eames, Church of Ireland Archbishop of Armagh

women to the Church of Ireland priesthood, in 1990 (the Church of Ireland took the his-toric step before all the other Anglican churches in the British Isles).

Eames has been forthright on public issues and as part of his work towards peace and reconciliation in Northern Ireland, he was notably involved in helping broker a Loyalist deal during the 1994 ceasefire. He was elected to the House of Lords as a Life Peer in 1995 – he sits as a cross bencher as the Most Reverend, the Lord Eames and is not tied to any political interest.

Eames has written a number of books, including *Through Suffering; The Church's Response to a Suffering Community* (1973). He is married to fellow Law graduate, Christine, and they have two sons.

James Ellis (as Norman) and Kenneth Branagh (as Billy) in the BBC Television play Too Late to Talk to Billy, *1980*

JAMES ELLIS *(1932–)* | Actor

James (or 'Jimmy') Ellis was propelled to the status of household name courtesy of the long-running television programme *Z Cars*. He was born in Gawn Street and spent his early life in East Belfast.

In the early 1940s he won a city scholarship to Methodist College, where he started acting. In 1950 he went to Queen's University to study English Literature, French and Philosophy, but abandoned his studies for the stage and became a member of the Belfast Arts Theatre, which was then situated in Fountain Street.

In 1951, aged 19, Ellis received a Tyrone Guthrie Scholarship to the Bristol Old Vic. He enjoyed his time in England, but was happy to come back to work at the Group Theatre. In the late 1950s he combined his talents of acting and directing when he became Artistic Director of the Group. He resigned that post in order to mount Sam Thompson's play *Over the Bridge* – an early attempt to address the problems of bigotry in working-class Belfast – which the Group directors had withdrawn from production. The play was staged at the Empire Theatre, Belfast, and broke all house records both there and later at the Olympia Theatre, Dublin.

In 1962, Ellis was chosen to play Sergeant Bert Lynch in *Z Cars*, a progressive and highly successful 'slice-of-life' BBC police drama that ran for a period spanning 16 years. Ellis's portrayal of the no-nonsense down-to-earth Lynch established the Ulster accent on the small screen for the first time. Amongst numerous other television appearances, he notably starred as the father in Graham Reid's *Billy Plays*, which also starred KENNETH BRANAGH. Ellis has also appeared frequently on the West End stage and enjoyed seasons at the National Theatre and with the Royal Shakespeare Company.

Ellis now lives in England, and is married with three children. He suffered a heart attack in 1999 in the midst of preparations for the television programme *This is Your Life*, which celebrated his achievements. Ellis also writes – following on from a book of verse, *Domestic Flight*, his book of short stories and translations *Home and Away* was published in 2000. He is currently completing his first novel, *Confirmed Bachelors*.

ST JOHN GREER ERVINE (1883–1971) | Novelist, Dramatist and Critic

St John Ervine, or John Greer Irvine, as he was named, was born in Isthmus Street, Woodstock Road on 28th December 1883, the son of deaf mute parents. One of the biggest early influences on him was his maternal grandmother who ran a shop on the Albertbridge Road.

In 1897, aged 14, Ervine went to work in an insurance company. Three years later he moved to London to take up the same employment. He joined the Fabian Society. His wife, Leonora Mary Davis was also a member. They married in 1911.

Ervine met W. B. Yeats, who was so impressed by Ervine's talent and industry that he smoothed the way for Ervine's first full length play *Mixed Marriage*, to be produced at the Abbey Theatre in 1911. In 1915 his play *John Ferguson* opened, and it later proved popular in America, as did his play *Jane Clegg*, staged in Manchester in 1913. Ervine managed the Abbey briefly in 1915, but his antipathy towards attitudes non-Northern led him to resign after the Easter Rising in 1916, much to the relief of Yeats.

He joined the Dublin Fusiliers, but was severely wounded during the First World War, and his leg had to be amputated. After the war, he moved to England and worked as a drama critic for *The Observer*. Ervine wrote more plays in the 1930s, returning to a local theme for his most famous work *Boyd's Shop* (1935). He became a member of the Irish Academy of Letters and from 1933 to 1936 was Professor of Dramatic Literature for the Royal Society of Literature.

Ervine also wrote biographies – of Sir EDWARD CARSON, Sir JAMES CRAIG (Craigavon), and George Bernard Shaw, for example – and novels. *The Foolish Lovers* (1920) and *The Wayward Man* (1927) are acclaimed. Nevertheless, he is best remembered for his Ulster comedies and his acerbic, controversial journalism. St John Ervine died in England (he had settled in Devon).

ANGELA FEENEY (1954–) | Opera Singer – Soprano

Angela Feeney is an international opera singer. Born on 19th October 1954 in Fort Street off the Springfield Road, she discovered her love of classical music at a cinema performance of *La Traviata* on a school trip at the age of 13. She began having singing lessons at the Belfast School of Music, winning all the major prizes at competitions throughout Northern Ireland. As a civil servant in Customs & Excise in Belfast, she funded her further studies at the College of Music in Dublin, where she travelled each weekend for lessons. In 1974, she moved to Dublin to concentrate full-time on her singing career and made her debut in 1977 with the Irish National Opera as Cherubino in *The Marriage of Figaro*.

She continued her studies in 1978 with a scholarship to the Richard Strauss Konservatorium in Munich. On completion of her degree, she was engaged by the Munich State Opera Studio for young singers. Her success led to a contract in 1982 as a soloist with the Munich State Opera – a first for an Irish soprano – where she worked with many renowned conductors. Feeney made her debut as Madame Butterfly with Opera Northern Ireland which she later repeated at the Berlin State Opera. In 1984, she made her English National Opera debut as Donna Elvira in *Don Giovanni*.

Feeney rapidly forged an exciting international career, appearing at the Hamburg and Frankfurt State Opera companies and throughout Europe. One of the highlights of her career was working with Leonard Bernstein at the Barbican Theatre, London, singing the role of Maria in *Westside Story*. She has made various recordings, including Rossini's *Stabat Mater* in 1997.

In 1994 she initiated the West Belfast Classical Music Bursary Awards, a competition open to all classical musicians born in Ireland, held in St Louise's Comprehensive College (see SISTER GENEVIEVE). These awards are now renamed the Belfast Classical Music Bursaries. Feeney continues singing throughout Europe, is Director of 'Allegro Belfast', which promotes classical musicians, and lives in Munich and Ballycastle with her musician husband and their son.

HENRY GEORGE (HARRY) FERGUSON *(1884–1960)* | Engineer and Inventor

Harry Ferguson, a man credited with revolutionising world agriculture, was born at Growelle, near Hillsborough, Co. Down in 1884. He left school at 14 to work on his father's farm, but soon became an apprentice in his brother's car and cycle repair business. Ferguson developed his own sports motorbike and a racing motor car. He was also the first man in Ireland to design and build his own aeroplane, which he flew on December 31st 1909.

In 1911, Ferguson opened his own car business in May Street, Belfast then moved to larger premises at 17 Donegall Square East. (The Ulster History Circle has erected a blue plaque to commemorate Ferguson at this address.) In 1914, he started to sell American tractors. The models were heavy and dangerous, so Ferguson designed and built a new plough which was coupled to the tractor in a three point linkage, so that tractor and plough formed a single unit. He patented this 'Ferguson System' which was to revolutionise farming, in 1926.

In 1938 he signed a deal with Henry Ford in Michigan, USA to sell a tractor of Ferguson's own design. Ferguson had a 'handshake' agreement with Ford in 1939, becoming the only partner Ford ever had (although Ford's grandson later reneged on the unwritten contract). The partnership produced 300,000 Ford Ferguson tractors, but ended in a law suit over patent rights held by Ferguson. Undaunted, Ferguson designed a new model, the TC-20, or 'Wee Fergie', which was built by the Standard Motor Company in Coventry. During ten years over 500,000 of these lightweight, inexpensive tractors were built.

Ferguson merged his company with the Canadian concern Massey-Harris to form Massey-Ferguson, which continues to supply tractors and agricultural machinery worldwide. A full-scale replica of Ferguson's aeroplane, and an early tractor and plough are on display at the Ulster Folk and Transport Museum.

This brilliant, innovative engineer died in Stow-on-the-Wold, Gloucestershire on October 25th 1960, a few days before his 76th birthday.

SAMUEL FERGUSON *(1810–86)* | Poet and Antiquary

Sir Samuel Ferguson was born on 10th March 1810. He lived in High Street and was educated at Belfast Academy, the Belfast Academical Institution and Trinity College, Dublin. Called to the Irish Bar in 1838, he took silk in 1859 and a Doctor of Laws in 1864.

Aside from his professional life, Ferguson was very interested in Irish culture. While still a lawyer he published a set of collected poems in 1865 entitled *Lays of the Western Gael*. Many of these poems were based on mythological cycles, indicative of Ferguson's interest in Irish folklore. Other poems, such as 'Willie Gilliland', reflected his Scottish Covenanters ancestry.

In 1867 Ferguson retired from practice, and moved to Dublin on his appointment as First Deputy Keeper of Public Records in Ireland. This work entailed a thorough reorganisation of this neglected department. His excellent work resulted in a knighthood in 1878.

Ferguson was responsible for much published material, including *Ogham Inscriptions of Ireland, Wales and Scotland*, and *Congal*, which was an epic poem in five books. He also wrote many essays on antiquities for the Royal Irish Academy, of which he was President in 1882. Ferguson's house in Great George's Street, Dublin was open to everyone interested in art, literature or music. *Poems of Samuel Ferguson* was published in Dublin in 1963.

Ferguson died in Howth, Co. Dublin on 9th August 1886 and was buried in Donegore, Co. Antrim. Like EDWARD BUNTING before him, his contribution to the recording of traditional Irish artforms cannot be underestimated.

VERE HENRY LOUIS FOSTER (1819–1900) | Philanthropist and Educationalist

Vere Foster did much to alleviate suffering during the famine years in Ireland. Born in 1819 in Copenhagen, Foster was the son of a British ambassador. He was educated at Eton and Oxford and was a British diplomat in South America from 1842 to 1847.

Foster visited Ireland in 1847 during the worst year of the Great Famine. He was appalled by the suffering he witnessed and decided he would help in whatever way he could. It is said he gave many emigrants their passage money, and he travelled on three emigrant ships to America, gathering information to secure reforming legislation. When famine threatened again in 1879, Foster promoted the emigration of women to America and the British colonies, assisting them financially.

Foster's contribution to education was immense. He secured grants to help construct several hundred new parish schoolhouses. He assisted in establishing a teacher's union and helped it develop into the Irish National Teachers' Organisation in 1868.

Perhaps he is best remembered for *Vere Foster's Copy Books* which consisted of handwriting, drawing and watercolouring. These books were published by the notable Belfast printers Marcus Ward and Company which started in Cornmarket in 1843, and moved to Donegall Place and finally to a purpose built factory on the Dublin Road as it expanded. The company had an office in London, and at one stage had 150 books in its catalogue. Foster's *Copy Books* were used in schools until the 1920s. He also wrote *The Two Duchesses*.

Foster moved to live in Belfast in 1867 and spent the rest of his life working for the relief of the sick and the poor, and virtually his entire fortune was spent on these causes. He died in Belfast at his house at 115 Great Victoria Street, on 21st December 1900. Only a few newspapers carried his obituary.

THOMAS GALLAHER (1840–1927) | Proprietor of Gallaher's Tobacco Company

Thomas Gallaher was the proprietor of what became the largest independent tobacco company in the world during the first decades of the twentieth century. He was born at Templemoyle near Derry/Londonderry in 1840. He began to process tobacco aged 17 and in 1863, he transferred the business to Belfast.

By 1891 there were 45 tobacco spinning machines at work in York Street, although it was not until 1902 that the firm started producing cigarettes. By then Gallaher's was employing over 1,600 people and was so busy that the company had a large factory in London to cope with the volume. Gallaher was an autocratic leader, constantly considering innovation and occasionally travelling to sample tobacco elsewhere to improve the product range. He also owned a tobacco plantation in America. Gallaher was Chairman of the Belfast Steamship Company, and became involved in the 1907 dock strike. Jim Larkin came from Liverpool to Belfast to organise the National Union of Dock Labourers, but Gallaher was determined to stamp out Larkinism. Events came to a head when Larkin infiltrated Gallaher's and organised the employees into a union. He referred to Gallaher as an 'obscene scoundrel'. Other workers came out in sympathy and there were riots on the Belfast streets that summer.

Gallaher died in Belfast in 1927 but Gallaher's continued to thrive, boosted during the depression of the 1930s when tobacco was regarded as a way of curbing appetite. In the 1950s, the firm still employed over 3,000 people, and it was only in the early 1980s that Gallaher's had to start reducing its workforce due to recession. The York Street factory – which was an important part of the social and economic history of North Belfast – was partly demolished in 1990, making way for the Yorkgate retail and entertainment complex. Gallaher's still operates a plant in Lisnafillin, Ballymena.

JAMES GALWAY *(1939–)* | Flautist

Sir James Galway, widely regarded as the world's leading flautist, was born in Carnalea Street, North Belfast, on 8th December 1939. As both his parents were musical, it was hardly surprising that young Jimmy (as he was known) showed great interest, first with the mouth organ and violin and then the flute.

Flautist James Galway, Belfast Festival at Queen's, 1980s

He played with the Onward Flute Band and the 39th Old Boys Band, and his potential was soon obvious. His father (a riveter at Harland & Wolff) made sure James received tuition and he joined the Belfast Youth Orchestra. A successful interview with the visiting John Francis of the Royal College of Music led to him leaving Belfast, aged 15, for London to study and practise at the Guildhall School of Music and the Royal College.

Galway won a scholarship to the Paris Conservatoire, where he found the lack of tuition disappointing, although he realised the benefits of his experiences there. In the early 1960s Galway grasped the chance to play lead flautist with the Sadler's Wells Company, London. He stayed for four years, but felt frustrated with the management and left to join the Royal Opera Orchestra at Covent Garden.

Galway won the City of Birmingham Symphony Stage Competition. As he'd just married, the prize of £1,500 was opportune. Buoyed by the prize, he left his job. Shortly afterwards the opportunity arose to play flute and piccolo with the BBC Symphony Orchestra which brought him into contact with Sir Malcolm Sargent, with whom he got on well.

Excellent press helped Galway develop his career. He was offered the job of first flute with the London Symphony Orchestra, followed by a spell with the Royal Philharmonic, and later session work. In 1969, he was interviewed by Herbert von Karajan for the highly regarded Berlin Philharmonic – he moved to Berlin in 1969. Galway found Berlin difficult at first, primarily because he didn't speak German. The prestige of the job, however, outweighed the downside.

In 1975, after some initial hesitation, Galway took the decision to go freelance. He embarked on a series of trips around the world, and also took up teaching posts in New York.

Galway has often returned to Belfast. He opened the Belfast Festival at Queen's in November 1976 with a concert at the Whitla Hall, and opened the Waterfront Hall's first concert in January 1997. Now based in Lucerne, and married to his third wife Jeanne, Galway has remained at the pinnacle of his profession for over 20 years. He was knighted in 2001 for services to music. The James Galway Scholarship has benefited several young musicians.

MIKE GIBSON *(1942–)* | Rugby International

Mike Gibson was an outstanding rugby player whose skill, pace and courage made him the world's most capped player, of his time. He won 69 caps for Ireland and showed his versatility by gaining 40 at centre, 25 at out-half and 4 on the wing. Gibson was part of an Irish team that made a record six wins in 1968; and was also an important part of Ulster's very successful interprovincial side of the late 1960s. He played for North Rugby Club in Belfast.

Born in Belfast in 1942, Cameron Michael Henderson Gibson grew up in the Cherryvalley area in the east of the city. He was educated at Campbell College, Trinity College, Dublin and Cambridge University. Gibson made his debut for Ireland while at Cambridge in February 1964. He played at out-half in a magnificent Irish win of 18–5 over England at Twickenham, the first since 1948 when JACK KYLE was at his peak.

Gibson made five appearances for the British Lions, three in New Zealand in 1966, 1971 and 1977, and two in South Africa – 1968 and the politically controversial but successful tour of 1974. The tour of 1971 saw the Lions defeat the All Blacks in a titanic struggle in which Gibson played a major part.

Gibson will long be remembered for his tactical awareness and speed of thought and reaction which allowed him to remain ahead of the game. Like all great sportsmen, he seemed to have time in which to make the next move; although he had great individual ability he always made best use of his talents to help the team. His vision made him an exceptional player and he last played for Ireland in Australia in 1979, finishing his international career on a high when Ireland won the two match series. He is a solicitor in Belfast.

FORSTER GREEN *(1815–1905)* | Philanthropist and Hospital Benefactor

Forster Green was a businessman and philanthropist who helped many worthy causes in and around Belfast in the 19th century. Born on 8th October 1815 in Annahilt, Co. Down, Green's family were Quaker linen merchants. (His brother William became a Quaker minister.) After attending Friend's School in Lisburn, he went into the family grocery business in Waring Street in Belfast.

After seven years he went to work for a tea and coffee merchant in Liverpool, and on his return to Belfast decided to set up his own tea company, aged only 22. After initial difficulties, Messrs Forster Green and Co flourished. He expanded the premises from 1 High Street (site of the 17th-century Markethouse where HENRY JOY MCCRACKEN was hanged in 1798) round into Cornmarket, and also set up a branch in Royal Avenue. Green acquired the High Street/Cornmarket site from Adam McLean and built his warehouse there in 1867. On the front of the building he placed a giant golden tea canister and a 'bright whirring coffee-grinding steam engine'.

As he became wealthy, Green's outlook began to change. He started his philanthropy with a donation of £2,000 towards the Society of Friends. He then turned his attention to health. He donated money to the Royal Victoria Hospital, helped the Throne (with a donation of £5,000 to establish a consumptive unit there) and Samaritan Hospitals, and bought

Fortbreda, enabling the Forster Green Hospital to move to its present site in South Belfast.

Green helped many local charities including homes for the blind and the Midnight Mission. The City YMCA and Shankill Road Mission both benefited from his generosity.

Green and his wife lived at Derryvolgie House on the Malone Road. On 21st October 1905 he died there after a short illness. He left £10,000 in his will 'for the respectable Protestant poor of Belfast, Down and Antrim'. He is buried at the Friend's Burial Ground on Balmoral Avenue.

HUGH HANNA *(1824–92)* | Presbyterian Minister and Educationalist

A controversial and outspoken Presbyterian minister, strong supporter of the Union and educationalist, 'Roaring' Hugh Hanna was born in 1824 in Dromara, Co. Down but he spent all his life in Belfast. He first worked as a teacher at various elementary schools and was ordained in 1852, beginning his work in a small mission hall in Academy Street.

Zealous and energetic, he did not go unnoticed for long, and was soon installed as minister of Berry Street Presbyterian Church, later rebuilt to hold an ever swelling congregation thanks to Hanna's charismatic style. As an orator, he had no equal. He often gave open-air sermons. When Daniel O'Connell came to Belfast, Hanna braved the riots and declared he would preach 'despite the Romish mobs'.

At a time in Belfast's history when tensions were running high due to the large number of rural workers who had poured into the city in search of work in the mills, Hanna was strongly behind the Conservative cause and during elections would speak on behalf of party candidates. He was strongly opposed to the Home Rule bills. In 1886, Belfast witnessed some of its worst ever riots. Some felt Hanna helped quell the disturbances in the Shankill Road area, while others felt his strident delivery and defiance of Rome from the pulpit did little to help. His sermons were always controversial, as were his letters to the press.

In 1872, Hanna moved to a larger, new church at Carlisle Circus, St Enoch's (now replaced by a much smaller church). He remained as minister of St Enoch's for twenty years. In 1885, he was appointed a Doctor of Divinity. Education was near to his heart, and he was instrumental in building school houses all over Belfast. St Enoch's had a Sabbath School, but Hanna also organised and managed day schools. He was also Commissioner of National Education for a time.

Hanna died of heart failure on February 3rd, 1892, at his home in Clifton Terrace, Duncairn Street. He was survived by a widow, two sons and four daughters. He left an undoubted mark on Belfast as witnessed by his funeral – thousands lined the streets at Carlisle Circus, Royal Avenue and Donegall Street as his hearse made its way from St Enoch's. His becloaked statue stood at the centre of Carlisle Circus until it was blown up in the 1970s.

SIR EDWARD HARLAND *(1831–95)* | Shipbuilder

Edward Harland was born in Scarborough, Yorkshire, and received a classical education at Edinburgh Academy. Harland wanted to be an engineer and got an apprenticeship with Robert Stephenson and Company in Newcastle upon Tyne. Harland then went to work with J. Bibby and Sons in Liverpool. He built up experience in shipbuilding and engineering in Liverpool and later on the Clyde. In 1854, he came to Belfast to work at Hickson's yard.

Working tirelessly for improvements, Harland was tough and uncompromising. He trimmed wages when necessary and banned smoking in the workplace. In 1857, he took on GUSTAV WOLFF as his personal assistant. A year later, Harland acquired Hickson's lease for £5,000 and soon started to build up the business. Bibby's placed orders (18 of the first 25

Sir Edward Harland, Bart., M.P., by Frank Holl (1884), Belfast Harbour Office

ocean-going ships were for Bibby's) and the Yard started to produce innovatory ships called 'Bibby Coffins' because of their flat bottoms and box shape.

On 26th January 1860 Harland married Rosa Wann, daughter of a wealthy businessman from Malone. On 11th April 1861, Harland and Wolff entered into partnership. Harland was the spokesman for the firm and the practical shipbuilder, dovetailing with Wolff's engineering and financial skills.

The early 1860s saw strong profits and high productivity. During 1871, the yard built the *Oceanic*, one of the first White Star liners, with a revolutionary design. In 1877 Harland became the Chairman of the Belfast Harbour Commissioners. The following year Harland & Wolff strengthened links with the Liverpool-based Asiatic Steam Navigation Company and expanded further by purchasing Alexander McLaine and Sons. Any profits crisis was always averted by a new order from the White Star Line or an innovation, like the triple expansion engine in 1884. Harland and Wolff had its own engine works in 1880 and in 1882 more slipways were added.

In 1885 Harland was appointed Mayor of Belfast. He became the biggest holder in the new limited company of Queen's Island Shipbuilding and Engineering Company Limited and also developed links with the West India and Pacific Steam Company. The Yard had entered its heyday; giant White Star liners came out of the yard regularly in the next thirty years.

In the late 1880s, Harland withdrew slightly from the business and got involved in politics. In 1887 he stood successfully for parliament as Conservative candidate for North Belfast. Harland sold his home Ormiston House in East Belfast, to WILLIAM PIRRIE and went to live in Kensington Palace Gardens, London, dubbed 'millionaire's row'. He received a Baronetcy for his services to commerce in 1885. When in Ireland he now resided at Glengorme Hall, Co. Leitrim.

In 1895 Harland was returned unopposed in the elections, but he died peacefully on Christmas Eve at Glengorme Hall, aged 64. His funeral on 28th December in Belfast was very well attended. Flags were at half mast and despite a strike at the time, the Harland and Wolff Yard was well represented. Early in 1896 William Pirrie became Chairman of Harland & Wolff. The shipyard, which at one time led the world as a centre for shipbuilding, began to lose money from 1964 on. It was privatised in 1989 and by the beginning of the 21st century had a workforce of a couple of hundred compared to 30,000 in its heyday. It still has the largest dry dock in the world and two of the tallest cranes, 'Samson' and 'Goliath', which tower above the city's skyline.

PAUL HENRY *(1876–1958)* | Artist

There can be few painters whose style is as familiar as Paul Henry's. His well defined studies of local people on Achill Island and his beautiful, serene Irish landscapes represent two separate phases.

Henry was born at 61 University Road, Belfast on 11th April 1876. His father was a Presbyterian minister (as was his grandfather) and life at home for Henry and his three brothers was rather strict and austere. After attending the Royal Belfast Academical Institution, Henry was apprenticed to the Broadway Damask Company as a textile designer. He found it boring, and enrolled for the Belfast College of Art. In 1898 he left for Paris to attend the Académie Julian. Influenced by the Impressionist school, Henry attended classes at James Whistler's studio. From 1900 he worked in London.

Paul Henry in his studio (painting a portrait of R.M. Henry)

In 1910 Henry's friend Robert Lynd suggested that he and his wife Grace join him on Achill Island. He fell in love with the island, and his empathy with its people and countryside is evident in his pictures, for example, *Launching the Curragh*. By 1920 he had moved to Dublin. Henry was a founder member of the Society of Dublin Painters, which included

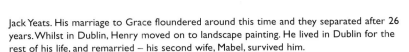

Jack Yeats. His marriage to Grace floundered around this time and they separated after 26 years. Whilst in Dublin, Henry moved on to landscape painting. He lived in Dublin for the rest of his life, and remarried – his second wife, Mabel, survived him.

Henry's pictures are constantly exhibited and his paintings are owned by all the major galleries of Ireland and the Victoria & Albert Museum in London. He died on 24th August 1958 in Bray, Co. Wicklow. Henry's remains are buried at St Patrick's Church, Enniskerry.

CHAIM HERZOG *(1918–97)* | Former President of Israel

Chaim Herzog was the sixth President of Israel, a position he held from 1983 until 1993 when he retired, aged 75. He was born in Belfast on 17th September 1918 at 2 Norman Villas (now 185 Clifton Park Avenue, where a plaque to his memory is placed), off the Cliftonville Road. The following summer his father left his ministry position in Belfast to move to Dublin where he became Chief Rabbi of Ireland. In 1935, the family emigrated to Palestine where his father was elected Chief Rabbi the following year.

Herzog, who studied Law in London and was called to the Bar at Lincoln's Inn in 1942, volunteered for service in the British Army. In 1946 he returned to Palestine, determined to help form the State of Israel. He joined the Haganah Jewish Underground and later became head of the Jewish Agency's security branch.

When the state formed, Chaim Herzog held several official positions. He was head of the IDF Intelligence Branch and was a general in the Israeli Army. In 1975, he was Israel's Ambassador to the United Nations. In 1981 Herzog was elected to the Knesset, or Parliament, as a member of the Labour party. In 1983, he was elected as President of Israel and was re-elected in 1988 for a second five year term. He died on 17th April 1997 in Tel Aviv, aged 78.

JOHN HEWITT *(1907–87)* | Poet

John Hewitt was a major figure in the local arts scene. Reminders of his legacy include the John Hewitt Summer School at Garron Tower, Co. Antrim, every August and a lively pub named after him in Lower Donegall Street, Belfast.

Born at 96 Cliftonpark Avenue in 1907, Hewitt attended Agnes Street National School (where his father was Principal), Methodist College and Queen's University, where he read English. He went on to become Keeper of Art at the Belfast Museum and Art Gallery (later the Ulster Museum) from 1930 to 1957, and this gave him an opportunity to get to know local artists and writers.

Hewitt's poetry was first published in left-wing journals like *The Irishman*. He went on to write two full collections and six pamphlets. In 1934 Hewitt married Roberta Black, Secretary of the Belfast Peace League, which they helped to found. The couple lived in several different houses in South

Portrait of John Hewitt by Basil Blackshaw (1984), Ulster Museum

Belfast in the course of their marriage.

Hewitt's many writings concentrated on folklore, custom, language and the human condition, topics he explored with a characteristic economic use of words. *Time Enough* (1976) won a Poetry Book Society Award. He also wrote a study of the weaver poets of Antrim and Down, entitled *Rhyming Weavers* (1974).

Although regarded by many as the 'father figure' of the current crop of Northern Irish poets, Hewitt's passion for the arts was evident in other directions too. He wrote books on art criticism, was a member of the Irish Academy of Letters and formed the 'Ulster Unit' of local artists (in 1934) with other luminaries including JOHN LUKE and COLIN MIDDLETON.

From 1957 until 1972, Hewitt was Director of the Herbert Art Gallery and Museum in Coventry. Back in Belfast upon retirement, he held the position of Director of the Lyric Theatre and was also the first writer-in-residence at Queen's from 1976 to 1979.

Hewitt remained active in the arts until the end of his life. He was no lofty intellectual, and always retained an interest in local life. *The Collected Poems of John Hewitt*, edited by Frank Ormsby was published in 1991.

ALEX HIGGINS *(1949–)* | Snooker player

Born in the Donegall Road district, Alexander Gordon Higgins spent much of his youth at the Jampot Snooker Club, where he developed into an excellent snooker player. He played for Northern Ireland at amateur level, before moving to England, and ended up at the World Championships of 1972 in Birmingham, playing world champion John Spencer.

Although *Pot Black* had started on BBC2 in the late 1960s, snooker was still a minority sport with a somewhat shabby image. Higgins pulled off a victory, won himself the princely sum of £480 and, it could be argued, changed snooker for ever. Suddenly, snooker had its own – often highly controversial – superstar. Snooker started to appear more on television, helped by the amount of colour sets being bought. Higgins became a great draw.

Higgins was runner-up for the world title in 1976 to Ray Reardon and in 1980 to Cliff Thorburn. Against the odds, Higgins won the title again in 1982. Anyone who saw his breathtaking victory over Jimmy White that year will never forget it. It was Higgins at his very best. Every time he got out of position, he managed to pot the next ball.

Higgins, who has been called 'Hurricane Higgins' and 'The People's Champion', was increasingly involved in disputes with the authorities and his form declined. In 1989, however, he became the first Northern Irish man to win the Benson & Hedges Irish Masters title.

Higgins returned to Belfast and now lives with his family back in the Donegall Road area.

DAVID HOLMES *(1969–)* | DJ and Musician

David Holmes started DJ-ing in the mid-1980s and has since spread his wings creatively to record albums, film tracks, TV themes and to entertain clubbers throughout the world. One of ten children, Holmes was born and brought up in the Ormeau Road area. He left school with few qualifications and worked as a chef in the Europa and Larry's Diner before joining Sax hairdressers.

All the while, he remained passionate about music. Sax helped him buy decks for £1,000 in the mid-1980s and he was on his way, DJ-ing firstly in the Abercorn and then in the Delta and Plaza. He mixed House and Dance music, and before long he was writing as well as sampling other material.

A collaboration called 'De Niro' with the Disco Evangelists led to 'Go! Disc' Records signing Holmes on a five record deal. *This Film's Crap, Let's Slash the Seats* was released in 1995. The album's blend of styles was well received, together with the stark black-and-white videos that accompanied it. Other albums followed, including *Let's Get Killed* in 1997 and *Bow Down To The Exit Sign* in 2000 which included collaborations with Bobby Gillespie, Jon Spencer, Martina Topley-Bird and David Arnold. Holmes, who has picked up several awards, still gigs in Belfast but spends much of his time DJ-ing worldwide or working on other creative projects.

In 1998/9 he was involved in a project at Mogwai on University Road, serving coffee and snacks into the early hours – the short-lived venue proved very popular with Belfast's weekend revellers.

Holmes has blended an instinctive feel for music with creative talent. His acclaimed soundtrack work has included the Steven Soderbergh films *Out of Sight* (1998) and *Ocean's Eleven* (2001).

BERNARD (BARNEY) HUGHES *(1808–78)* | Baker, Reformer and Philanthropist

Bernard Hughes came to Belfast as a poor labourer in 1826. By the 1870s he owned the largest baking and milling enterprise in Ireland. Hughes was also an industrial reformer, politician and Catholic lay spokesman, and was renowned for his liberalism. Born in Armagh in 1808, he started work as a baker's boy aged 12. Moving to Belfast, he got a job in a small bakery in Church Lane and subsequently worked in the Public Bakery in Church Street.

At 21, he married a Presbyterian, Jane. They were married by the legendary HENRY COOKE, with whom Bernard enjoyed convivial relations for years to come. In 1833, Hughes became operations manager for the Public Bakery, and in 1840 he opened his own bakery in Donegall Street, living in nearby Lancaster Street.

In the 1840s he was recognised as Belfast's leading master baker. He spoke out against poor working conditions, and was instrumental in abolishing Sunday and night baking – bakers started work at 5 a.m. rather than 11 p.m. In 1846 he opened a bakery at 15 Donegall Place and constructed a railway line to ease delivery over the cobbled streets to Fountain Lane; it was known as The Railway Bakery.

The Great Famine brought terrible hunger to Belfast and Hughes responded by producing a cheaper household loaf which helped alleviate an appalling situation. He also introduced Barney's 'bap', which was famed in the Belfast children's song 'half a bap with sugar on the top'; anyone with the surname Hughes in Belfast came to be nicknamed 'Bap'.

Sadly, his wife died aged 44. She is buried at Friar's Bush graveyard. After her death, Hughes invited his three sons into the business. Edward, the youngest, became the first Chairman of the *Irish News* and also managed the bakery for many years. In 1849, Hughes married his second wife, Margaret Lowry. They had three daughters. In 1850, he opened his third bakery, in Divis Street.

In the 1850s, Hughes also turned to politics. He became the first Catholic member of the Belfast Corporation and represented Smithfield Ward on the Town Council. The ward was the scene of rioting and shootings in 1857. Hughes gave evidence to the Royal Commission, and also continued to act in disputes between bakers and their employees. In 1863 he welcomed the Bakehouses Regulation Act which improved hygiene and safety standards. He stood as a Liberal candidate in the 1871 election and remained Liberal councillor for Smithfield, and became the first Catholic to be elected an Alderman for the Town Council.

Hughes worked into his late sixties, supported by Edward. He died on 23rd September 1878, and was buried in Friar's Bush. He is remembered for his business vision, liberalism and resoluteness in the face of opposition from local hierarchy. He is also remembered for his philanthropy – for example, donating the ground on which St Peter's Cathedral was built and donating money to build St Mary's Hall, Bank Street (now demolished). Bernard Hughes and Company produced bread at Springfield Road until June 1979, when the business was wound up.

OTTO JAFFE (1846–1929) | Lord Mayor of Belfast, Businessman and Benefactor

Otto Jaffe, a well-known and important figure in late Victorian Belfast, was the only Jewish Lord Mayor yet to preside in the town. He was born in Hamburg on 13th August 1846. In 1850 his father came to Belfast to establish a linen exporting business and Otto was educated in Holywood, near the family home.

In 1877 Jaffe took over the family firm. He married Paula Hertz from Brunswick in 1879, and they had two sons. The firm flourished under Jaffe's shrewd eye. He also threw his energies into public life. He was a member of the Harbour Board and a Governor of the Royal Victoria Hospital. A member of the Senate at Queen's, he contributed £4,000 to fund the University Physiology Laboratory.

Jaffe was first involved in local government as a city councillor in 1894. He became Lord Mayor in 1899, and was knighted at the end of his term, principally for his charitable work. Lord Mayor again in 1904, Jaffe also held the post of High Sheriff of Belfast. He contributed financially to the building of a new synagogue in Annesley Street, near Carlisle Circus – now used as a physiotherapy centre by the Mater Hospital. (The first synagogue in Belfast was built at 113 Great Victoria Street in 1871, incidentally beside VERE FOSTER's last home. When the new synagogue opened in Annesley Street in 1901 the old building became an Orange Hall and then an Apostolic Church; it was demolished in 1993.) Jaffe also helped set up a school for Jewish children on the Cliftonville Road. This school, the Jaffe Centre, was burned down in the mid-1990s. Otto Jaffe died on 29th April 1929 in London.

MARIE JONES (1951–) | Playwright

Marie Jones, born in East Belfast, the daughter of a Harland & Wolff shipyard worker, is an award-winning playwright of international repute.

Jones began acting with JAMES YOUNG at Belfast's Group Theatre and started writing in a collective in the early 1980s. She was writer in residence at the Charabanc Theatre Company between 1983 and 1990, and her first play, co-written with the renowned Belfast writer Martin Lynch (who did much to encourage her at the outset of her career), was Lay Up Your Ends. Further plays followed for Charabanc, including Gold in the Streets and Somewhere over the Balcony.

Jones later worked for Replay and Dubbeljoint theatre companies, producing plays such as Yours Truly, A Night in November and Stones in his Pockets, which won the Irish Times/ESB Award for best production of 1999. Jones' husband, Ian McElhinney, directs Stones in his Pockets, which has been translated into 25 languages including Hebrew, and in 2001 directed the world premiere of the musical version of her play Weddins, Weeins and Wakes at the Lyric Theatre as part of the Belfast Festival at Queen's. Stones in his Pockets enjoyed a longstanding run at the Duke of York's Theatre in London's West End in 2001/2, earned her the Laurence Olivier Award and had a successful run on New York's Broadway.

Her play Ruby about local singer RUBY MURRAY proved controversial, but also very popular and toured Northern Ireland after a run at the Group Theatre. Her direct, comic style has deservedly won Jones plaudits and she is now one of the most respected contemporary playwrights. She often takes a local situation and gives it a twist of comedy or drama to add spice.

Jones has received the John Hewitt Award for Contribution to Cultural Traditions, and in 2000, won the Special Judges' Award as part of the Belfast Arts Awards for her lifetime contribution to the arts in the city. She has also been awarded an honorary doctorate from Queen's.

A picture of Marie Jones appears on the bottom left of the front cover.

FRANCIS JOY (1697–1790) | Founder of the *News Letter*

Francis Joy has the distinction of founding the *News Letter*, the oldest newspaper in Ireland and the oldest surviving news-sheet in Europe.

Born in 1697 in Belfast, Joy was one of the Belfast's early printers. In records of the time, he was described as a 'conveyancer and notary public who was given a printing works to pay off a debt'. Once well established, the printer and papermaker founded the *News Letter* in 1737 at The Sign of the Peacock building; the full title of the paper was the *Belfast News Letter and General Advertiser*. It was first published in Bridge Street, then in Joy's Entry (and later in the 19th century in Donegall Street and currently off Boucher Road). Throughout most of the 18th century, the newspaper was published on Tuesdays and Fridays and consisted of four pages, packed with news, advertisements, comment, poetry and parliamentary reports. Joy employed few editorial staff and was often forced to rely on virtually every scrap of news that came his way. The paper reflected his radical, liberal stance.

In 1745, Joy handed the *News Letter* over to his sons Robert and Henry. Francis started a paper mill in Randalstown – he was the first paper-maker in Ulster – and retired in his fifties, a wealthy man. He died in 1790.

The Joys were related to the McCrackens (see HENRY JOY McCRACKEN and MARY ANN McCRACKEN) and the families lived next door to each other in High Street. Robert and Henry Joy became joint editors of the newspaper, and also owned Cromac Paper Mill.

Francis Joy's grandson, Henry Joy was born in 1754. He started work in the *News Letter* in 1782 and became its editor in 1789; he was also owner of Joy's Paper Mill. He was not a supporter of the United Irishmen and joined the Yeomanry when the 1798 rebellion broke out. In 1794 he jointly published *Belfast Politics; A Collection of Debates, Resolutions and Other Proceedings in the Town 1792 and 1793*. He was also the anonymous author of *Historical Collections Relative to the Town of Belfast* in 1817. Henry Joy died in 1835.

BRIAN KEENAN (1950–) | Writer

Brian Keenan's name is etched on public consciousness due to the four and a half years he was held hostage by fundamentalist Shi'ite militia in Beirut, Lebanon.

Born in East Belfast in 1950, Keenan left school at 15. He worked with a heating firm in East Belfast, and studied for a City and Guilds qualification as a heating engineer.

Not feeling fulfilled, Keenan went to night school where he started to blossom, winning prizes for poetry. He went on to the University of Ulster where he took a degree in 19th- and 20th-century Irish, British and American Literature, followed by an MA in Anglo Irish Literature. Keenan worked as a teacher in Belgium, Spain and Belfast, where he was also involved in community development. In 1985 he went to Beirut to lecture in English, but was kidnapped and held captive until August 1990. His experiences are recounted in his best selling account, *An Evil Cradling*, where he describes how he and fellow hostage John McCarthy were kept in darkness and regularly beaten.

Keenan's release came after diplomatic intervention by Irish Foreign Affairs Minister Gerard Collins. Keenan disliked the limelight and was pleased when the publicity died down. *An Evil Cradling* was acclaimed, receiving the *Irish Times* Prize for non fiction, the Christopher Ewart-Biggs Memorial Prize, the *Time Life* International Prize and the Christopher Award, New York. He was awarded the CBE in 1992 and an honorary degree from Queen's for services to humanity followed.

In May 1993, he married Audrey Doyle, a Dublin physiotherapist who had helped nurse him back to health. His sisters, Brenda Gillham and Elaine Spence, were given the 'People of the Year Award' in Dublin in 1990. They had campaigned tirelessly for his release from captivity.

Keenan has continued to pursue his literary career. He was writer in residence at Trinity College, Dublin, in 1993 and took a Fellowship in English there in 1994. *Between Extremes*, a travelogue about Patagonia, was published in 1999, and was followed by a fictional study on the life of the ancient Irish harper Turlough Carolan, *Turlough* (2000).

BRIAN KENNEDY *(1966–)* | Singer

Brian Kennedy is one the most exceptional vocal talents to have emerged from Belfast. Not only a prolific songwriter, he is a master interpreter of lyrics. Born in the Beechmount area of the Falls Road, he left Belfast for London when he was 18, where he gigged in bars and lived with Belfast musician friends 'The Adventures' for a time.

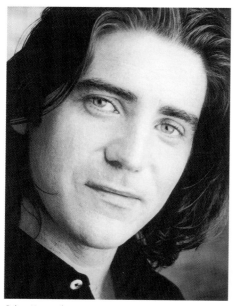

Brian Kennedy

Kennedy secured a contract in 1991 with RCA Records. He released *The Great War of Words* as a solo album. Songs like 'Captured' and 'Town' became immediate favourites, especially with live audiences.

Performing live has always been at the core of Kennedy's success. VAN MORRISON, on hearing Kennedy's voice, immediately invited him to perform as part of his blues and soul revue which travelled the globe and culminated in the double live album *A Night in San Francisco* featuring the late John Lee Hooker. Kennedy contributed to Morrison's live shows and studio albums, such as *No Prima Donna, Days Like This, The Healing Game* and *Back on Top*, and Morrison executively produced Kennedy's version of 'Crazy Love' which featured in the movie *When a Man Loves a Woman*. Kennedy also joined Morrison in a duet for the official visit of US President Bill Clinton to Belfast in 1996.

Kennedy has toured with Tina Turner, The Bee Gees, Suzanne Vega and Everything But The Girl, amongst others, and taken his solo show all over the UK, Europe, Australia and New Zealand. He has also worked with the 'Fifth Beatle', Sir George Martin, performing classic Beatles songs as part of a live concert series which was broadcast on RTÉ.

On March 16th 2000 he made his Broadway debut in *Riverdance on Broadway* at the Gershwin Theater, singing songs specially composed for him by Bill Whelan. Kennedy went on to play 290 performances, eight times a week, in the sold-out production.

Kennedy's album *A Better Man* led to an Irish Music Industry Award for 'Best Irish Male Album' and a Hot Press/2TV award for 'Best Irish Male Artist'. His double CD *Won't You Take*

Me Home…The RCA Years, featuring previously unreleased recordings, was released in 2000, and the album *Get On With Your Short Life* was released in 2001, strengthening his reputation as an artist with a distinctive musical vision.

Brian Kennedy's brother Bap Kennedy has also enjoyed musical success. His critically acclaimed albums include *Domestic Blues*, *Hillbilly Shakespeare* and *Lonely Street*.

WILLIAM DOOLE KILLEN *(1806–1902)* | Presbyterian Minister and Writer

The Reverend Doctor William Doole Killen was a Presbyterian minister of note, as well as a writer on church matters. Born on 5th April 1806 in Ballymena, he was descended from pioneers of the Scottish Presbyterian movement associated with the Plantation.

He was educated in Ballymena, at the Belfast Academical Institution and at Trinity College, Dublin, where he studied Classics. Ordained in 1829, he became minister of Raphoe. In 1841 he succeeded the renowned HENRY COOKE as President of the Theological College in Belfast, appointed by the General Assembly.

His Chair at the College included remits on Ecclesiastical History and Pastoral Theology. This breadth of knowledge inspired him to write a number of volumes including *The Ancient Church*, *Old Catholic Church* and *Ecclesiastical History of Ireland*. He was known for his plain and concise style.

Killen was responsible for raising £11,000 towards new collegiate buildings and two new manses, during his presidency. He was known to present sermons in a forceful, Calvinistic style.

Killen retired from the Assembly in 1889. His brother was minister of First Comber Presbyterian Church, and his uncle, T.Y. Killen, D.D., was also a renowned churchman.

Killen was married to a Miss Young, and they had three boys and a girl. After a very short illness, Doctor Killen died on 10th January 1902, at the venerable age of 95.

JAMES KIRKPATRICK *(c.1670–1744)* | Presbyterian Minister, Physician and Writer

Dr James Kirkpatrick was important to Presbyterianism's development in Belfast and beyond. Ordained in 1699, he became minister of First Presbyterian Church, Rosemary Street. He was also a member of the Belfast Society, a physician in his latter years, and a writer of some note.

Kirkpatrick was the son of Hugh Kirkpatrick, who was a minister in Lurgan, Ballymoney and Dalry and Old Cumnock in Scotland. James was born in Scotland and in 1691 he graduated from the University of Glasgow. He moved to Templepatrick, Co. Antrim where he served as a minister from 1699 to 1706.

In the early 18th century Presbyterianism was in a state of flux. Kirkpatrick became one of the earliest members of the Belfast Society in 1705. The group was broadminded; many were clergy who agreed on man's individual right to reason, and several were well in advance of their times.

In 1706 Kirkpatrick was appointed Assistant to John McBride of the Belfast Church. The congregation increased to such an extent that a new meeting house was built, and Kirkpatrick became minister of the second congregation. The new church, Second Presbyterian, built in 1708, was erected at the rear of First Presbyterian. (The roof of the church was used as a meeting place for the United Irishmen in the 1790s, and in 1813 it was the setting for the first Belfast performance of Handel's *Messiah*, with EDWARD BUNTING as organist and with a full orchestra.) It was knocked down in the 1960s and a car park now occupies the site. In 1712 Kirkpatrick was elected Moderator of the Synod of Ulster.

In 1720, members of the Belfast Society, including Kirkpatrick, decided that candidates for the ministry should not be required to subscribe to the Westminster Confession of Faith. The Synod reacted by deciding all such non-subscribing ministers should separate off; they subsequently formed the Non-Subscribing Presbytery of Antrim. In other words, Kirkpatrick fell considerably from grace due to his position. Ironically, life had started to improve for the Presbyterian Church which had gone through a turbulent passage for much of the 17th century – in 1718 George I had restored the 'regium donum' in the Irish Toleration Act, and increased it to £2,000 per annum.

Kirkpatrick continued as a minister, but also qualified as a physician. He also wrote a number of works, including *A Historical Essay upon the Loyalty of Presbyterians in Great Britain from the Reformation to this Present Year 1713*. Published and printed anonymously, it is thought that the printer JAMES BLOW (see PATRICK NEILL) was responsible. *An Account of the Mind of the Synod* was published anonymously, by 'A Lover of Truth and Peace'. His work *A Defence of Christian by a Member of the General Synod* was left unfinished. His printer and friend, Blow, prefaced the book with an explanation about the author's sudden death in Dublin.

A copy of Kirkpatrick's portrait hangs in the vestry of First Presbyterian Church.

JACK KYLE *(1926–)* | Rugby International

Jack Kyle was one of the greatest Rugby Union out-halves in the world during the 1940s and 1950s. Capped 46 times by Ireland, he inspired the country to three championships and two triple crowns between 1948 and 1951.

Born John Wilson Kyle on 10th February 1926, he grew up off the Cavehill Road in North Belfast and attended Belfast Royal Academy. He excelled at all sports at school, including cricket and boxing. He liked studying arts subjects but concentrated on Science when he decided to study Medicine at Queen's. Time constraints as a medical student forced him to drop cricket, but rugby brought him recognition while he was still at college. Aged 19, Kyle played for Ireland against the British Army in December 1945. The following year, he played in several 'Victory' internationals, making a considerable impression.

Kyle made his debut for Ireland in 1947 and soon became a regular. Between 1948 and 1951 he was simply outstanding, masterminding the Irish triumphs of that era. In 1950, he toured with the British Lions to New Zealand. He excelled in both defence and attack. Not only could Kyle read the game well, but he had excellent hands and a fine turn of speed. Kyle played for Ireland until 1958, and was a member of the first Irish team to beat a touring side when Australia went down 9–6 at Lansdowne Road in 1956.

Many accolades have followed his marvellous career. He was awarded the O.B.E. for services to rugby, and was elected to various rugby Halls of Fame in Belfast, Dublin and London.

Kyle worked in Zambia as a surgeon for many years, where he took the position of Vice President of the Zambian Rugby Union. Now retired, he lives in near Newcastle in Co. Down.

SIR CHARLES LANYON *(1813–88)* | Architect and Civil Engineer

Many of Belfast's most imposing buildings were designed by Sir Charles Lanyon, who was also responsible for some of the Ulster's early railway lines.

Lanyon was born in Eastbourne in 1813. After a private school education, he was articled to Jacob Owen of the Irish Board of Works in Dublin, to prepare to be a civil engineer. In 1835, he took second place in the Irish County Surveyorship exams. He also married Owen's daughter, Elizabeth Helen.

Lanyon worked as County Surveyor of Kildare before moving north. In Co. Antrim, he constructed the Coast Road from Larne to Portrush, and designed the Belfast–Ballymena railway line, as well as engineering the Belfast–Holywood–Bangor line. Lanyon was also responsible for Belfast's Queen's and Ormeau Bridges, and from the mid-1840s set about constructing some of the most famous landmarks in Belfast architecture.

In the late 1840s, Lanyon completed Queen's College (later University) and the County Courthouse and Gaol on the Crumlin Road. The west façade of Queen's (now known as the Lanyon Building) is one of Belfast's best-loved landmarks and, with its accomplished massing and fine neo-Tudor detail, represents the best of Victorian revivalist architecture. The Union Theological College in Botanic Avenue, which he built in 1852–3, is a Renaissance Revival building replete with Roman Doric columns and Corinthian columned screens. Lanyon was also responsible for the striking Palm House in Botanic Gardens and also designed the grand house at Ballywalter Park for ANDREW MULHOLLAND, the Belfast industrialist.

Lanyon often worked with William Henry Lynn, as in the case of Belfast's fine Custom House, built in the 1850s in Italian Renaissance style. The duo often worked together on churches – St Patrick's Church of Ireland in Jordanstown, for example, blends Celtic-revivalist and Roman influences. Lynn designed Belfast Public Library in Royal Avenue and the Memorial Methodist Church in Carlisle Circus. The firm of Lanyon, Lynn and Lanyon (with junior partner John Lanyon drawing up the plans) was responsible for the Scottish-Baronial Belfast Castle built for the Donegalls (see SIR ARTHUR CHICHESTER) on the Antrim Road.

In the 1860s, Charles Lanyon diversified his career. He resigned the County Surveyorship and was elected Mayor of Belfast in 1862. Four years later he was returned as one of the Members of the Borough.

In 1862, Lanyon was elected President of the Royal Institute of Architects of Ireland, a position he held until 1863. He was also a Fellow of the Institute of British Architects and a member of the Institute of Civil Engineers. He was knighted in 1868. Lanyon died at his house, the Abbey, Whiteabbey on 31st May 1888 and was buried in Newtownbreda church-yard. His wife pre-deceased him and his son William, later Sir William Owen Lanyon, became a colonial administrator of note.

SIR JOSEPH LARMOR *(1857–1942)* | Physicist

Sir Joseph Larmor was a distinguished physicist whose innovative work helped prepare the way for Einstein's Theory of Relativity. Born in Magheragall, Co. Antrim, on 11th July 1857, Larmor attended the Royal Belfast Academical Institution and Queen's College before furthering his studies at St John's College, Cambridge, attaining a first and the award of Smith's Prizeman.

Larmor was appointed Professor of Natural Philosophy at Queen's College, Galway in 1880. He returned to St John's College in 1885 as a lecturer in Mathematics. In 1903, he was appointed to the distinguished position of Lucasian Professor of Mathematics in Cambridge.

He wrote a number of papers published in the *Philosophical Transactions of the Royal Society*, on the subject of 'A Dynamical Theory of the Electric and Lumeniferous Medium'. This was later revised and put into book form in 1900 under the title *Aether and Matter*. This was Larmor's main achievement. He was the first person to provide a formula for the radiation of energy from an accelerated electron. Larmor also researched the effect of a magnetic field on the spectrum.

Larmor was knighted in 1909. He was awarded the Royal Medal and Copley Medal in 1921. Larmor was also Unionist MP for Cambridge University between 1911 and 1922. He was granted the Freedom of the City of Belfast and had numerous honorary degrees bestowed upon him.

Larmor returned to Northern Ireland when he retired. Unmarried, he died in Holywood, Co. Down, on 19th May 1942.

SIR JOHN LAVERY *(1856–1941)* | Artist

Lavery was born in Belfast on 17th March 1856, the son of Henry Lavery, a publican on the corner of North Queen Street/Sussex Street. When the wine and spirit trade failed in 1859, Henry sailed to America to seek his fortune, but tragically the ship sank. Three months later John's mother Mary died, leaving John and his two siblings orphans. He was dispatched to his Uncle Edward and Aunt Rose's farm (called 'The Back of the Wood' and later changed to 'Train View' when railway lines were laid) in Moira, Co Down. John attended the local school for some years, and spent his youth in Moira and Ayrshire where other relatives lived.

Lavery secured a job as an apprentice retoucher of photographs in Glasgow. It was to his liking, and he earned enough to register at the Haldane Academy of Art in Glasgow. He subsequently set up as an artist; his debut exhibition at the Glasgow Institute of Fine Arts in 1880 was well received and he was soon offered regular work.

Lavery attended the Académie Julian in Paris where he developed the *pleinairiste* style close to Impressionism (particularly evident in *Under the Cherry Tree* in the Ulster Museum – he donated over 30 paintings to the collection). He made frequent trips to France, Tangiers and Switzerland, constantly honing his style and broadening his experience. Back in Scotland, he was part of the group of artists dubbed 'The Glasgow Boys'. Work became frequent and Lavery found himself moving in wealthy and socially élite circles. He moved to London in 1896 and lived at 5 Cromwell Place. He was knighted (in 1918), awarded honorary degrees from Queen's and Trinity College, Dublin, and made a Freeman of both Dublin and Belfast.

Lavery became renowned as a portrait painter, depicting Winston Churchill, Eamon de Valera and the tenor John McCormack among others. He was also commissioned to record key events of the Irish Civil War; Lavery's American-born wife, Hazel, was highly emotionally involved with the Irish cause, and had a liking for Michael Collins. Lady Lavery was an attractive socialite, and her face adorned Irish banknotes for many years.

Lavery continued to paint in his latter years, but his work became less refined. The year before his death he published his autobiography, *The Life of a Painter*. He died, aged 85, in Kilkenny, leaving a marvellous legacy of beautiful paintings, on exhibition all around the world. Lavery presented his first religious painting, *The Madonna of the Lakes*, a splendid triptych of the Blessed Virgin Mary, St Patrick and St Brigid, to St Patrick's Church in Donegall Street in 1917 (where it still hangs) – Lavery had been baptised in St Patrick's on 26th March 1856.

C.S. LEWIS *(1898–1963)* | Novelist, Critic and Christian Apologist

Clive Staples ('Jack') Lewis was born in Dundela Avenue, Ballyhackamore. He was baptised in St Mark's, Dundela, by his grandfather, the Reverend Thomas Hamilton, who was the Rector. Poet, philosopher, novelist, Lewis mastered every literary form with ease during his career. He was also a man who wrestled with his conscience, guilt and issues of Christian theology.

He read voraciously as a child, and wrote imaginative stories with his brother Warren. Lewis's mother died young, and his father sent him to Malvern College boarding school in England. He returned during the summer vacations, often playing in the Holywood Hills. Wounded at the Battle of Arras, Lewis returned from the army to University College, Oxford, where he achieved a Triple First and became a fellow and tutor of Magdalen College. Heinemann published his first volume of poetry and he continued writing, as well as tutoring and undertaking research. He became a committed Christian aged 30; a decision that heavily influenced his life and writing.

At Oxford, he met J.R.R. Tolkien, on whom he tested much of his work. Lewis's popularity as a lecturer gave him the confidence to write. *Out of the Silent Planet* (1938), ostensibly a science fiction novel, explored the struggle between good and evil, and man's ability to adapt to new and difficult circumstances. His first commercial success was with *The Screwtape Letters*, a blend of humour and philosophy. BBC broadcasts on religion also proved popular. As with his books, he gave much of the proceeds of his work to charity.

Sculpture by Ross Wilson of C.S. Lewis opening the wardrobe door to Narnia, Newtownards Road

During the Second World War, evacuees stayed at the Lewis household (which he shared with his brother Warren and an old family friend, Mrs Moore). Jack liked children, and, deciding to 'meet children as equals', he drafted *The Lion, the Witch and the Wardrobe*. Tolkien did not like it, but the book, published in 1949, was very well received. A series of seven Narnia books followed on the theme of children in a mythical land overcoming the forces of evil. Spiritual, mythical and religious undercurrents run through the stories, which can be read as biblical allegory.

Lewis became friendly, through correspondence, with the American Joy Davidman Gresham. Unhappily married with two sons, she came to England in 1953. Following her divorce, the couple married in a registry office, followed later by a religious ceremony. Joy became ill with cancer and, despite a period of remission, she died in 1960. She partly inspired Lewis' autobiography *Surprised by Joy*.

Lewis found it hard to recover from Joy's death. Now Professor of Mediaeval and Renaissance Literature at Cambridge (although he still lived outside Oxford), he continued to work. His faith stayed with him; *Letters to Malcolm, Chiefly on Prayer* (1963) was his last book. On November 22nd 1963, Lewis died, following a short illness and was buried at Holy Trinity Church, Haddington, Oxford. His relationship with Joy Gresham was the subject of the film *Shadowlands*.

A sculpture of Lewis and his wardrobe stands outside the Holywood Arches Library, Belfast (where there is also a short history of his early life in the area). C.S. and Warren Lewis presented a window to St Mark's Church, Dundela in memory of their parents, in 1935.

MICHAEL LONGLEY *(1939–)* | Poet

Longley, recipient of the T.S. Eliot Prize and the Hawthornden Prize for *The Weather in Japan*, published in 2000, is a major figure in national and international literary circles. His collection *Gorse Fires* was awarded the Whitbread Prize for Poetry when it was published in 1991. Born in Lower Crescent, Longley was educated at the Royal Belfast Academical Institution and Trinity College, Dublin, where he read Classics.

Longley taught in Dublin and London before returning to Belfast, teaching at Inst. He worked for the Arts Council from 1971 to 1991, where his remit included Literature, Traditional Arts and Arts in Education.

During the 1960s, Longley was involved with 'The Belfast Group'. Instigated by lecturer Philip Hobsbaum and based at Queen's, this group of poets included Seamus Heaney and Ciaran Carson. Meetings and wide-ranging discussions later took place at Heaney's house in Ashley Avenue and the Four in Hand pub on the Lisburn Road.

Longley's first volume, *No Continuing City* was published in 1969. *Selected Poems* (1998) showcased the output of a poet who once declared that he 'writes when he has something to say'. His achievements to date speak for themselves.

Longley is a Fellow of the Royal Society of Literature and a founder member of the Cultural Traditions Group. In March 2000, Belfast City Council marked the poet's 60th birthday by commissioning a portrait by Jeffrey Morgan for permanent display in the Waterfront Hall.

Longley lives near the Lisburn Road in South Belfast. His wife Edna Longley is a critic and Professor of English at Queen's. They have three children.

JOHN LUKE *(1906–75)* | Artist

Probably best known for *The Three Dancers* painting (in the Ulster Museum), John Luke was a talented landscape and portrait artist. He was born on 16th January 1906 at 4 Lewis Street off North Queen Street in Belfast. One of eight children, he worked for Workman Clark shipbuilders (see SIR GEORGE CLARK)when he left school.

After being injured at work, Luke enrolled for evening classes at the Belfast School of Art in 1923–4. He made immediate progress which led to a free scholarship for 1924–5. Teaching Art part-time, he continued to advance and was awarded the Sorella Local Art Exhibition prize of £50; winning the Dunville Art Scholarship of £100 a year in 1927 gave him the security to apply for Slade School of Art, and he left Belfast for London in 1930.

Luke secured a Diploma in Fine Art from Slade, and came back to Belfast in the early 1930s. In 1933 he took part in an exhibition of the Northern Ireland Guild of Artists. He also began sculpting.

The war years were lean, but the late 1940s saw one man exhibitions organised by the Belfast Museum at Stranmillis (now the Ulster Museum, where JOHN HEWITT, with whom Luke was friendly, was Keeper of Art) and the Council for the Encouragement of Music and the Arts (CEMA). His work took on an ethereal, spiritual phase, as evidenced in *Madonna and Child*.

In the 1950s Luke taught part-time at the College of Art. The Belfast Museum commissioned a mural *The Rehearsal* and later work included a mural at the Technical College's Millfield site. He also painted the mural on the inside of the City Hall's dome to mark the 1951 Festival of Britain (see p3).

Luke moved from Westland bungalows to a flat at 240 Duncairn Gardens. Ill health had made him delay some work, and eventually he was forced into hospital. He died in the Mater on 4th February 1975, aged 69.

John Luke's work is far from forgotten. The Arts Councils of Ireland arranged an almost complete collection of his work for display at the Ulster Museum and Douglas Hyde Gallery in 1978, and the Bell Gallery in Adelaide Park held a 'work from the studio' exhibition in 1980 in honour of this eclectic artist.

JAMES MACKIE JUNIOR and THOMAS MACKIE | Industrialists

Started by Scot James Mackie in 1858, Mackie's became one of the biggest firms in Belfast outside the shipyards by 1900 and found a niche market in producing machine tools during the Second World War.

James Mackie came from Scotland to install steam engines at a flax spinning mill in Drogheda. When in Ireland, he accepted the post of Manager at James Scrimgeour's Belfast textile machinery works. When the company got into difficulties, Mackie stepped in and took over the Albert Street Foundry in 1858. At first there were only a few employees engaged in turning spindles and repairing textile machinery, but it wasn't long before Mackie introduced work on flax cutters and twisting and spinning frames, and by 1862 there were around 100 wet spinning frames on the premises. James Mackie realised his company had a niche. Belfast's growing linen and, latterly, shipbuilding industries meant an on-the-spot engineering foundry was a real boon.

In 1887 James Mackie died. Shortly afterwards his sons took over the business, continuing with the same dynamic approach as their father. James Mackie Junior and Thomas Mackie acquired a four-acre site on the Springfield Road in 1893 to boost the output of both machinery and castings.

Soon the export business was flourishing. By the early 1920s, Mackies had branched out into jute machinery manufacturing and in the 1930s and 1940s developed its range further to become leading suppliers of sisal and hard-fibre spinning machinery as well as new types of machinery for spinning synthetic fibres and wool.

During the Second World War, Mackies produced armour piercing shells, and machine tools for munitions. The company continued to be busy into the 1960s, employing over 6,000 people at the end of the decade. The employees were producing a wider range and a greater volume of machines than during the heyday of textile engineering.

James Mackie Junior, who had lived at one time at 'Marietta House' on the King's Road, died in 1943, and gradually the direct family influence started to diminish. In 1977, the family relinquished control to a Charitable Trust. When Gordon Mackie resigned as chairman at the end of the 1980s, the family link had ended. Global recession meant Mackies had to down-size. By 1981, only 3,200 people worked at the plant. The following few years witnessed a rough ride for the concern. A revival under Pat Dougan in 1995 and a Queen's Award for Export the same year was very positive, together with a stock exchange quote, but eventually losses brought this historic concern down and in 1999, receivers were appointed.

Mackies has an important place in the industrial history of Belfast, and as an employer in the Springfield Road area.

JAMES MAGENNIS *(1919–86)* | Victoria Cross winner

James Magennis (or McGinnes – the spelling on his birth certificate; it was misspelt when he joined the Navy and he did not change it) was one of only three junior ratings awarded a V.C. in the Second World War. He was born in 4 Majorca Street off the Grosvenor Road, and attended St Finian's Junior School and De La Salle Brothers. He joined the Royal Navy in 1935.

After training and serving on *The Kandahar* he was selected for submarine work. An excellent swimmer, Magennis took to the job of diver, and in 1942 he joined the X Craft

Special Service. In 1945 Magennis was detailed to 'Operation Struggle' to target the 10,000 ton Japanese cruiser *Takao*, which guarded the entrance to Singapore Harbour. Despite a leak in his diving apparatus, Magennis made his way to the cruiser, scraped off barnacles and attached six mines. Because the mine carrying mechanism wouldn't disengage, he had to go back. Seven minutes later, his task was complete and six hours later, *Takao* exploded.

Both Magennis and his Commanding Officer, Lieutenant Fraser, were awarded the V.C.; Magennis receiving his from King George VI at Buckingham Palace in December 1945. Magennis received a hero's welcome in Belfast, and a fund was started for him, which amounted to over £3,000, a very considerable sum. this was presented to him by the Lord Mayor Sir Crawford McCullough, in front of cheering crowds.

In 1946 Magennis married Edna and they had four boys, one of whom was killed in a motoring accident in 1952. Magennis' naval career tailed off and he left the Navy in 1949.

Back in Belfast, he worked at the RN Air Station, but times were hard and he was forced to sell his V.C. for £75. Viscount Furness stepped in to return it, but Magennis had to endure the glare of newspaper publicity. Magennis also had to cope with feeling shunned by sections of his own Catholic community because of his British honour.

In 1955, disillusioned with life in Belfast, the family moved to Yorkshire, where Magennis worked as an electrician. He was happy with the obscurity of living in first Rossington and then Bradford, and when he died in July 1986 in the Halifax Infirmary, a plaque was erected in his honour in the local Anglican parish church.

Belfast artist George Fleming campaigned to have Magennis honoured in his native city. His campaign proved successful, resulting in the unveiling of a memorial in the grounds of the City Hall after Belfast City Council voted in favour in February 1997. Lieutenant Fraser V.C., almost 80, attended the unveiling of the bronze and Portland stone plinth, shaped like a ship's capstan.

One sad footnote prevails, however – Magennis's surviving sons sold their father's V.C. for £31,900 because, it is said, they could not afford to insure it (the first Royal Navy V.C. to be sold at public auction – at Sotheby's in London).

ROBERT SHIPBOY McADAM *(1808–95)* | Gaelic Scholar and Antiquarian

Also known as a local man of letters, Robert Shipboy McAdam established the Soho Engineering Foundry in Townsend Street in 1832 with his brother James.

Born in Belfast in 1808, into a Presbyterian middle-class household, McAdam was educated at the Belfast Academical Institution. He is said to have spoken and written 13 languages and been familiar with many more. He was certainly fluent in Gaelic, publishing a Gaelic Grammar and collected Irish manuscripts, and founding the Ulster Gaelic Society, the first language revival organisation of its kind in Ireland.

McAdam was also heavily involved in Belfast's burgeoning 19th-century arts and literature scene. He was the principle founder of the *Ulster Journal of Archaeology* in 1853, and edited the publication for nine years. He was also a member of the Belfast Literary Society, the Belfast Natural History and Philosophical society, the Linen Hall Library and the Harmonic and Harp Societies.

Robert McAdam died in 1895 and is buried in Newtownbreda. He lived in College Square East – a plaque has been erected on the present building, Stokes House, to commemorate him.

THOMAS McCABE *(1740–1820)* and
WILLIAM PUTNAM McCABE *(1776–1821)* | United Irishmen

William Putnam McCabe was one of the major figures in the United Irishmen of 1798, although his activities and influence lasted into the 19th century. His father, Thomas, was a watchmaker (at a jewellery shop in North Street) and well-known liberal thinker, and was involved in the meetings with Wolfe Tone in 1791 that led to the formation of the Belfast Society of United Irishmen in Peggy Barclay's Tavern in Crown Entry, off High Street. The McCabe house, 'The Vicinage' on the Antrim Road, was also a meeting place for the group.

William McCabe became involved with the United Irishmen newspaper *The Northern Star*. In 1794 the Attorney General filed a libel action against McCabe and several others for the paper's seditious material. William lent his talents to the campaign in the south, organising Kildare, Wexford, Carlow, Tipperary and Westmeath in 1796. Due to his endeavours, 279,000 men in Ulster, Munster and Leinster took the United Irishmen oath before the struggle began. Arrested in Dublin in May 1798, he managed to bluff his way out of jail and participated in the rebellion before escaping to England where he promoted the uprising in Manchester and London. He moved to France but found it difficult to whip up support in Paris. He then moved to Rouen where he tried unsuccessfully to establish a cotton factory. Disillusioned with Bonaparte's tepid attitude towards the Irish movement, he left France in 1803.

He returned to Ireland for a while before travelling to Scotland. Everyone seemed satisfied with this arrangement. Whitehall was pleased that McCabe was not in England and the Irish administration was happy he was living outside their jurisdiction. Much of his life was spent in Scotland.

In 1814 however, McCabe was arrested after entering Ireland illegally. Although the Uprising was well in the past, McCabe was still considered a danger and was refused permission to stay. He was escorted out of the country by the Chief Police Officer after Chief Secretary Robert Peel granted him pardon retrospectively on condition of permanent exile. William McCabe died in 1821.

HENRY JOY McCRACKEN *(1767–98)* | United Irishman

Born on the 31st of August 1767, Henry Joy McCracken was from a wealthy Presbyterian family, living in High Street, then the hub of Belfast's burgeoning commercial life. His father, a sea captain, owned the town's first large ropeworks. Henry Joy was put in charge of a cotton factory owned by the family on the Falls Road aged 22 and lived in the area for a while.

Many of the leading Belfast mercantile families were liberal Presbyterians. They were offended by the treatment meted out to the town's Catholic minority by the Anglican establishment. The French Revolution, reported in the *News Letter* (before any other British paper) – which was founded by McCracken's uncle Francis Joy – fired up these Belfast radicals.

As a result, the United Irishmen formed in 1791 in Peggy Barclay's Tavern, reputedly in Crown Entry off High Street, and resolved to 'form themselves into an association to unite all Irishmen to form a cordial union amongst all people of Ireland'. Dr William Drennan was the originator of the group and its first president and Wolfe Tone, a politically active Dublin lawyer, gave it its name; other activists were Thomas Russell and James Napper Tandy. Tone arrived in Belfast at the group's second meeting and soon inspired them to take action. In 1792, they launched their newspaper *The Northern Star*, edited by Samuel Neilson, a draper from Waring Street.

Reform proved very slow over the next few years. With no hope of peaceful change, the United Irishmen began to prepare for revolution. In 1795, Tone came back from France and met McCracken, Russell and others on Cave Hill, where they swore allegiance to the cause. Tone also promised help would be forthcoming from France, and the United Irishmen launched their offensive against the Government's forces.

Portrait of Henry Joy McCracken, 1767–98, by Sarah Cecilia Harrison (1926), Ulster Museum

The conflict in June 1798 occurred in counties Antrim and Down and McCracken accepted the mantle of Commander of the Northern Forces of the United Irishmen. After several skirmishes, the United Irishmen were defeated. McCracken, who led the attack at Antrim, escaped the battlefield and hid out on Slemish and Cave Hill in the Gamekeeper's cottage. The daughter of the cottage's owner, Mary Bodell (or Bothwell) had a daughter by McCracken. She was later adopted by his sister MARY ANN MCCRACKEN as her mother sailed for America – it was rumoured that she had been secretly married to McCracken.

McCracken was captured outside Carrickfergus, court martialled at the Exchange in Waring Street and held in the Donegall Arms Hotel in High Street. When he refused to inform on his fellow insurgents, he was tried, convicted and hanged at the Markethouse on the corner of Cornmarket and High Street on 17th July 1798. Mary Ann, herself a radical, comforted him before the hanging and had a doctor waiting at their house in case the body could be revived; the story goes that she was prevented from keeping a lock of his hair. Simultaneously, Henry Munro (see FRED ALDERDICE), the leader of the Lisburn insurrection, was hanged in Lisburn's Market Square.

McCracken's body was buried in the grounds of the Corporation Church (on the site of present-day St George's Church in High Street). During building work in the area, FRANCIS JOSEPH BIGGER removed what he believed to be McCracken's bones, and reburied them at Mary Ann's grave in Clifton Street Graveyard.

MARY ANN McCRACKEN (1770–1866) | Philanthropist

Mary Ann McCracken was the sister of HENRY JOY MCCRACKEN. Born on 8th July 1770, she lived in High Street at a time when Belfast's wealth and power was held by a handful of families. Their mother's family, the Joys (see FRANCIS JOY), owned a large cotton factory and had founded the *News Letter*.

She attended David Manson's progressive co-education school in Donegall Street. While still in her teens, she set up a small muslin business which she ran with her sister Margaret. The McCrackens were interested in cultural pursuits, and Mary Ann was one of the original members of the Belfast Harp Society. The renaissance in Irish harp music was largely due to the enthusiasm of EDWARD BUNTING, who lived with the McCrackens for many years.

In 1791, Mary Ann's brother helped establish the United Irishmen in Belfast, aided by Wolfe Tone's arrival from Dublin. For the next 12 years, she was closely associated with radical politics, and contributed to her brother's thoughts on social reform. When Henry Joy was hanged (with five others) after the 1798 uprising, Mary Ann accompanied him to the scaffold in Cornmarket on July 17th. She managed to get his body intact (the others were drawn and quartered and their heads put on spikes on the Market House) and take it to their house where a doctor was waiting; they were, however, unable to revive him and he was buried in High Street graveyard, site of the old Corporation Church (present-day St George's). She had financially supported him and lobbied hard for his life, and she did the same for fellow insurgent Thomas Russell, with whom she fell in love. Nothing came of the romance as Russell was hanged in Downpatrick for his part in an abortive uprising in 1803. Afterwards she withdrew from politics. After Henry's death, and in the face of

Mary Ann McCracken, social reformer, and sister of Henry Joy McCracken

opposition, she adopted his illegitimate daughter Maria and brought her up in the family home in Rosemary Street. She later lived at 62 Donegall Pass (where an Ulster History Circle plaque marks the house).

For the next ten years, Mary Ann concentrated on her muslin business, until an economic downturn in 1813 forced her to close it down. She subsequently became a force in the Ladies' Committee of the Belfast Poorhouse. There she remained as Secretary for more than 15 years. She was especially concerned with the education of destitute children. Philanthropic work was to dominate the rest of her life – she was active in the Society for the Relief of the Destitute Sick and in the Belfast Ladies Clothing Society. She also wrote regularly, and contributed much to Doctor Madden's seven-volume collection *A History of the United Irishmen*.

Mary Ann McCracken also campaigned for the abolition of slavery and to improve the lot of factory workers. She kept up her interest in social work almost until she died, aged 96. Her body is buried in Clifton Street Graveyard, the grave marked with a stone inscribed 'Wept by her brother's scaffold' and '*Dileas go h-eag*' (Faithful unto death).

DENNIS McCULLOUGH *(1883–1968)*
Irish Republican & Co-founder of the Gate Theatre

Born in West Belfast in 1883, Dennis McCullough became head of the Irish Republican Brotherhood (IRB) Supreme Council in 1914 and was one of the main instigators of the Republic's formation.

McCullough was educated by the Christian Brothers. He joined the Gaelic League in 1900 and in 1903 he joined the IRB. He wrote pamphlets and articles with Robert Lynd and Bulmer Hobson, who founded the Protestant National Association.

It was felt that the Republican movement was rather stagnant. To revive it, McCullough and Hobson launched the Dungannon Clubs which soon had branches all over the country. On the suggestion of Maire Butler, EDWARD CARSON's republican cousin, the Clubs merged with other organisations to form Sinn Féin. By 1914, the Northern Republicans controlled the IRB as McCullough ousted the Dublin leadership and became head of the Supreme Council.

In 1916, McCullough led the Irish Volunteers. Although imprisoned at various stages during the conflict, he was freed by 1918 and was elected as a Sinn Féin Councillor to the Belfast Corporation.

For some months McCullough sat in the Dáil (under Cosgrove's control) for a Donegal constituency. After partition, McCullough settled in Dublin. He founded the Gate Theatre with Michael MacLiammoir and was Chairman of the New Ireland Assurance Company until he retired in 1964.

Once the Republic of Ireland was established, he took on the role of diplomat. He went to the United States as Ireland's representative, and was Ireland's delegate at a commercial conference in 1927 in Rio de Janeiro, Brazil. He also attended an international Labour conference in 1936. McCullough was a director of ten major Irish companies, including Clondalkin and Killeen paper mills. He died in Dublin.

WAYNE McCULLOUGH *(1970–)* | Boxer

Known as 'The Pocket Rocket', former WBC Bantamweight champion Wayne McCullough is one of the best boxers to have emerged from Belfast and he is justly feted when he returns to his native city.

McCullough was born on 7th July 1970 in the Shankill area of the city. Two of his brothers boxed and he followed them to the Albert Foundry gym. Of 200 amateur fights, McCullough lost only 10. He represented Ireland in 50 internationals, and his glittering amateur career peaked with a Gold Medal at the 1990 Commonwealth Games, a Bronze at the 1990 World Cup and a Silver at the 1992 Olympics.

In September 1992, McCullough signed a contract with American promoter Mat Tinley and relocated to Las Vegas where he worked with the renowned trainer, the late Eddie Futch. His early bouts went well, and in January 1994 he won the NABF title in only his 11th fight. In July 1995 he won the WBC Bantamweight title after travelling to Nagoya, Japan, to take the title from the champion in his home town. He vacated the belt before moving up in weight to challenge for the WBC Super Bantamweight title in 1997.

He has challenged, albeit unsuccessfully, for another three world titles. He fought Daniel Zaragoza for the WBC Super Bantamwright title in January 1997, but lost in a controversial split decision. He took Naseem Hamed to twelve rounds for the WBO Feather-weight title in October 1998, and went the distance with Eric Morales in a close fight in 1999. A brain scan before a fight in 2000 has caused McCullough to take a career break, however, leading neurosurgeons have since cleared him and he is expected to challenge for a world title again.

JAMES McDONNELL *(1763–1854)* | Founder of Belfast Dispensary and Fever Hospital

Doctor James McDonnell was one of the founders of the Belfast Dispensary and Fever Hospital, which eventually became the Royal Victoria Hospital. (The Belfast Dispensary started off in Clifton House funded by the Belfast Charitable Society. The Fever Hospital in Frederick Street was opened in 1817; it became the General Hospital and then the Royal Hospital and only closed down when the Royal Victoria Hospital opened on the Grosvenor Road in 1899.) McDonnell also lobbied for and pioneered the provision of medical facilities for the poor.

Born in Cushendall in 1763, McDonnell studied Medicine in Edinburgh, graduating in 1784. He returned to Belfast to work and opened a dispensary in 1792. In 1797, he became involved in the Hospital Planning Committee's plans to open a hospital in a house in Factory Row, which is where Berry Street now stands. Initially only the house belonging to a Mr Pollard was rented, which contained six bedsteads, but in due course three houses in West Street at the corner of Smithfield were bought as the hospital expanded. Doctor McDonnell was one of the attending physicians. Records show the hospital closed briefly to allow him to recover from a bout of fever.

In the 1820s, Doctor McDonnell's rounds included Donegall Place, Rosemary Street, Church Lane and Cromac Street. He pressed hard to improve conditions for the mill workers in the area. He often gave talks, expressing hopes for a medical school in Belfast.

McDonnell had many other interests. He was a founder of the Linen Hall Library, and a member of both the Belfast Literary Society and Belfast Natural History Society. He was a personal friend of many of the United Irishmen, including HENRY JOY MCCRACKEN and Wolfe Tone. He was also involved in the Belfast Harp Festival of 1792 held at the Assembly Rooms in Waring Street (the building, dating from 1769 still exists, in the form of the old Northern Bank).

PATRICK McDOWELL *(1799–1870)* | Sculptor

Patrick McDowell is best remembered for the original 'Black Man' statue of Frederick Richard, Earl of Belfast, which started life in College Square East and now resides in Belfast City Hall.

McDowell was born in Belfast in 1799. He was educated at a school run by engraver Hugh Gordon. He went to London with his mother and was apprenticed to a coach-builder. While in London, he lodged with a French sculptor Peter Francis Chenu, who taught him to draw and sculpt. Under his influence, McDowell became an accomplished sculptor.

He first came to public attention with his work *The Girl Reading*, and he exhibited at the Royal Academy in 1822. Before long McDowell was receiving many sculpture commissions, including the Elder and Younger Pitts, and Viscount Fitzgibbon of Limerick.

On the 1st November 1855, his statue *Frederick Richard, Earl of Belfast*, (the 'Black Man'), was erected in front of the Royal Belfast Academical Institution. Frederick Richard, only son of the Donegalls, was a romantic Victorian figure who died of Scarlet Fever in Naples aged 26 – a talented poet and musician, he had also been an advocate of popular education. McDowell's scuplture was the town's first public statue, perhaps an indication that Belfast was starting to take itself seriously as a cultural and commercial centre. The statue was moved to the Old Town Hall in Victoria Street in 1874 to make way for HENRY COOKE'S statue and was later moved to the City Hall.

McDowell's other work included a memorial to William Tennent in First Presbyterian Church in Rosemary Street. His final sculpture was *Europa*, commissioned for the Albert Memorial in Kensington Gardens, London. McDowell died in London in 1870.

WILLIAM FREDERICK McFADZEAN *(1896 –1916)* | Posthumous winner of the Victoria Cross

Private William Frederick McFadzean was awarded a posthumous V.C. for his actions during the Battle of the Somme in the First World War.

Born in Lurgan, Co. Armagh but moving to Belfast as a youngster to live at 'Rubicon House' at 372 Cregagh Road, McFadzean was a strong, well-built Collegians rugby player who joined the 14th Battalion of the Royal Irish Rangers.

At the Somme he was detailed as a bomber due to his build. It meant he had the dangerous job of going over the top carrying buckets full of hand grenades. As the battalion prepared for attack near Thiepval Wood on July 1st 1916, grenades were being prepared and some of the soldiers were crowded around the ammunition box when it fell to the ground and two safety pins fell out. McFadzean knew what was going to happen, so he threw himself on the box before it exploded. He was killed instantly, but his brave action saved many other lives.

A V.C. was gazetted on 9th September 1916 and his father William was presented with it at Buckingham Palace on 28th February 1917.

There is no known grave for McFadzean, although his bravery is commemorated at the Thiepval Memorial as well as Newtownbreda Presbyterian Church, First Lurgan Presbyterian Church, Collegians Rugby football Club and Castlereagh Borough Council.

BARNEY McGLONE (ROBERT ARTHUR WILSON) *(1820–75)* | Journalist

Robert Arthur Wilson, who wrote under the pseudonym of Barney McGlone, was a journalist with Belfast's *The Morning News*. He was the most popular and widely read journalist of his time. *The Morning News* had its premises at 6–10 Crown Entry in Belfast. Bought over by the proprietor of the *Freeman's Journal* in 1884, the paper was finally absorbed by the *Irish News* in 1892.

Wilson was born in Falcarragh, Co. Donegal. The son of a Donegal coastguard, he spent some years in America. His mother wanted him to become a Methodist minister, but he had his heart set on writing. He worked for *The Nation* and for Enniskillen newspapers on his return from America, but he really made his name, or rather his pseudonym, in *The Morning News*.

The newspaper often sent him on roving reports. In 1859, he attended the centenary celebrations of the birth of Scottish poet Robert Burns in Ayr, and wrote a poem 'The Bard of the Poor'. McGlone also published a volume of verse in 1874. In 1875, he was sent by *The Morning News* to cover the centenary of Daniel O'Connell's birth in Dublin, but he died of a heart attack while he was there.

McGlone was so popular with the public that his readers erected a small monument to him in the Belfast City Cemetery on the Falls Road where he is buried. He was a colourful, flamboyant character who walked about in a large black hat and cravat. Legend has it that he even once deputised as a clergyman and preached eloquently in Manorhamilton Methodist Church.

MEDBH McGUCKIAN *(1950–)* | Poet

Medbh McGuckian is a renowned poet who was born in Belfast in 1950 and educated at Dominican College and Queen's University. After her primary degree in English, she took a Masters in Irish Writers and Gothic Fiction. She went on to teach English at Dominican College and St Patrick's College, Knock.

McGuckian has published a number of collections, including *Single Ladies* (1980), *Flower Master* (1982), *On Ballycastle Beach* (1988) and *Captain Lavender* (1994). Her lyrical, esoteric style balances emotion and reality.

McGuckian was writer in residence at Queen's University during the 1980s. Since 2000, she has been involved in teaching the Masters in Creative Writing at Queen's.

SIOBHÁN McKENNA *(1923–86)* | Actress

Siobhán McKenna was born into a Gaelic speaking household in Belfast in May 1923. The family moved to Galway in 1928 and she attended University College, Galway from 1940 to 1944. She made her stage debut at Galway's Gaelic Theatre in 1940. After graduating, she moved on to the Abbey Theatre in Dublin to appear in productions including *The Countess Kathleen*. McKenna married fellow Abbey Theatre player Denis O'Dea in 1946.

McKenna soon built up an international reputation. Her first London production was in *The White Steed* in 1947 and she appeared on Broadway, New York, as the lead in George Bernard Shaw's *Joan of Arc* in 1956. In 1959, she successfully tackled the male role of *Hamlet*.

She gave notable performances in her few film appearances; which have included *Playboy of the Western World* (1962) and *Doctor Zhivago* (1965). In America she was possibly best known for her appearances in the television anthology *Hallmark Hall of Fame*.

McKenna was made President of Ireland's Advisory Council of State in 1975. She received many honours, including an honorary doctorate from Trinity College, Dublin, and life membership of the Royal Dublin Society in 1983.

BERNARD MacLAVERTY *(1942–)* | Writer

Initially known for his short stories, Bernard MacLaverty is now equally renowned for his novels, many of which have been set locally. Born in Belfast in 1942, he lived in Atlantic Avenue off the Antrim Road until the late 1960s. He worked at Queen's University as a laboratory technician for over ten years before taking a degree at Queen's and moving to Scotland.

MacLaverty taught in Edinburgh and then moved to the Isle of Islay off the west coast of Scotland. His *Secrets and Other Stories* was published in 1977. It received a Scottish Arts Council Book Award.

He wrote two other acclaimed volumes of short stories after making another break-through with *Lamb*, his first novel, about a Borstal run by religious brothers. Well received, Liam Neeson took the lead role in the film adaptation. *Cal* was published in 1983. Set in Northern Ireland, it deals sensitively with a love affair between a young terrorist and the widow of his victim. John Lynch and Helen Mirren starred in the 1984 film.

MacLaverty wrote the script for *The Real Charlotte* and has written children's books. In 1997, his beautifully-crafted *Grace Notes* was short-listed for the Booker Prize – this novel confirms his considerable talent, as does his most recent, *The Anatomy School*, published in 2001.

Bernard MacLaverty now lives in Glasgow with his wife and family.

MICHAEL McLAVERTY *(1904–72)* | Novelist

Michael McLaverty was a writer of intricate, sensitive short stories and novels, mostly set in rural Northern Ireland. Born in Carrickmacross, Co. Monaghan on 5th June 1904, he moved to Belfast with his family in 1909. His mother Catherine died young but his father Michael stayed in Belfast, working as a waiter in the Queen's Café in Queen's Arcade.

Michael was educated at St Malachy's College before graduating from Queen's as a Bachelor of Science in 1927. He took a higher diploma in education and became a Master of Science in 1933. He started teaching in 1929 at St John's Public Elementary School in Colinward Street, West Belfast. McLaverty married fellow teacher, Mary Conroy, and together they had four children. Later he became headmaster of St Thomas's Intermediate on the Falls Road.

A keen sportsman, it wasn't until he suffered an injury that he started to read seriously. One thing led to another, and Michael McLaverty was soon putting pen to paper. His early works *Call My Brother Back* and *Lost Fields* are semi-autobiographical. Sets of short stories about rural life followed, such as *The White Mare* and *The Game Cock*. His novels *The Three Brothers* and *The Brightening Day* are about ordinary people in their local communities, told in precise style.

A revival of interest in McLaverty's work occurred in the late 1970s. *Collected Stories* was published in 1998 and Poolbeg Press launched a reprint series together with a volume of his uncollected works.

In the early 1960s, the renowned poet Seamus Heaney taught for a year at St Thomas's – McLaverty encouraged the young teacher to write.

ROBERT McLIAM WILSON *(1966–)* | Novelist

The chain-smoking, wise-cracking writer Robert McLiam Wilson was most recently celebrated when his novel *Eureka Street* was serialised on BBC television. He was born in 1966 and brought up in West Belfast. He attended St Malachy's College before going to Cambridge University to study English.

McLiam Wilson then went to London to start work on his first novel *Ripley Bogle*, which was published in 1989 and brought him to the attention of a national and international audience. The story is about an intelligent, confident homeless person with views on terrorism, politics and life in general who hits the streets of London. *Ripley Bogle* won the Hughes Prize, the Rooney Prize, the Irish Book Award and the Betty Trask Award.

McLiam Wilson followed this with *Manfred's Pain* in 1992. He returned to his Belfast roots with *Eureka Street* in 1996 about a rather unprepossessing Protestant protagonist called Chuckie Lurgan who comes up with a brilliant, if dubious, business idea. The book forms a savage satire on the 'peace dividend' of 1994 and the grant system. His novel *The Inflatable Citizen* was published in 2001.

Besides his novel writing, he has worked with the writer Carlo Gébler on a television documentary entitled *The History of the Baseball Bat*.

McLiam Wilson's is a fresh talent and he writes with spark, wit and originality. He is married and lives in South Belfast.

LOUIS MacNEICE *(1907–63)* | Poet

Frederick Louis MacNeice is probably best remembered for his poetry, but his talents encompassed drama, lecturing, travelogues, features work and BBC wartime scriptwriting. He was born in Brookhill Avenue, Belfast when his father was Church of Ireland Rector of Holy Trinity, Clifton Street. The family moved to Carrickfergus in 1909, when his father was appointed Rector there. Like C.S. LEWIS, a contemporaneous Belfast writer, MacNiece's mother died young, but his father re-married, and there was a strong rapport between stepmother and son; MacNeice was also close to his sister, Elizabeth.

MacNeice went to Sherbourne and Marlborough public schools in England, followed by Merton College, Oxford, where he gained a double first. There he formed lasting friendships with Stephen Spender and W. H. Auden (with whom he later wrote *Letters from Iceland*). He published his first set of poems *Blind Fireworks* in 1929. Shortly afterwards, he became Assistant Lecturer in Classics at Birmingham University. He married in 1930 and had a son, Dan, but the marriage did not last.

In 1936, he obtained a lectureship in Greek at the University of London. *Modern Poetry* and his classic poem 'Autumn Journal' were published, the latter regarded as a kind of political harbinger of the forthcoming conflict. In 1940, he was asked to write propaganda scripts by the BBC, which later led to a staff position. At this time, MacNeice met and quickly married a singer called Hedli Anderson. He wrote a play called *Christopher Columbus* with a musical score by William Walton. This was followed by the much acclaimed play *The Dark Tower* which was an allegory for the ending of the Second World War.

In 1950 MacNeice became Director of the British Institute in Athens, where he organised a lively programme of cultural events. This he did along with a fair amount of partying, which he continued on his return to London. Much of MacNeice's work for the BBC in the 1950s revolved around travel features which afforded him relief from his increasingly troubled marriage to Hedli. In 1960 his marriage broke up and MacNeice moved in with Mary Wimbush, who stayed with him for the rest of his life.

MacNeice's last years brought a certain temperance to his active socialising. He wrote new plays and poetry and lectured at Cambridge. He had been planning features on rural matters when he caught viral pneumonia in August 1963 and died shortly afterwards.

MacNeice has been described as 'the poet's poet', finding a meeting point between total accessibility and an intellectual standpoint. He was influenced by T.S. Eliot's imagist style, and, like Eliot, attacked many aspects of bourgeois society and modern life. Despite living mostly in England, he was conscious of his background: 'I was born in Belfast/between the mountain and the gantries/To the hooting of the sirens and the clang of horns' he wrote in 'Carrickfergus'. He is buried at Carrowdore, Co. Down, beside his mother and grandfather. His autobiography *The Strings Are False* was published posthumously in 1965.

COLIN MIDDLETON *(1910–83)* | Artist

Born at 48 Victoria Gardens, North Belfast, on 29th of January 1910, Middleton was the son of a damask engineer. In 1927 he went into his father's trade and studied simultaneously at the Belfast School of Art.

In 1935 he was made an Associate of the Royal Ulster Academy and exhibited for the first time at the Royal Hibernian Academy in 1941; Middleton exhibited at the Bell Gallery and Arts Council as well as many times in Europe. During the Second World War, JOHN HEWITT, Keeper of Art at the Belfast (later Ulster) Museum, arranged for a large one-man show of his work; the public was highly impressed by his range, with Tom Carr describing the show as 'an amazing anthology of modern art'.

Middleton attributed his feelings for texture to his training for the damask business. Influenced by Van Gogh, his style could be described as a mixture of bold expressionism and the primitive, leaving a wonderful legacy of landscapes, figures and street scenes.

Until 1970 Middleton worked as a school teacher, but an Arts Council award when he was 60 enabled him to devote himself full time to painting. He worked steadily until he fell ill with leukaemia. Middleton died in Bangor, Co. Down, on December 23rd 1983 aged 73. He was survived by his second wife, Kathleen (née Barr) and two daughters. (His first wife, the artist Mae McClean, died young.) The Ulster Museum and Arts Council both own several of his works.

ALEXANDER MITCHELL *(1780–1868)* | Inventor of the Screw Pile

Alexander Mitchell invented the screw pile, described as a patent that 'made him famous and has been used by engineers all over the world ever since'. It was certainly crucial to the development of Belfast as a major port. He was born on April 13th 1780, the son of William Mitchell, Inspector General of Barracks in Ireland.

Mitchell became a civil engineer. Despite being almost blinded by a severe bout of smallpox aged 22, he carried on a successful brick-making and building business in Belfast until 1832. He invented machines to improve brick-making, and, in 1842, patented the Mitchell screw pile and mooring, as a new method of constructing lighthouses in deep water and on mud banks and shifting sands. The patent also advanced the fixing of beacons and mooring of ships. The screw pile was used for the building of lighthouses at Morecambe, the Thames estuary and Belfast Lough, and the system also helped in the construction of viaducts and bridges for the Bombay and Baroda railway lines.

In 1837, Mitchell was elected Associate of the Institute of Civil Engineers, and as a full Member in 1848. His improved method of mooring ships was adopted by many authorities. The Corporation of Newcastle upon Tyne purchased its use for £2,500.

Mitchell retired in 1857. Initially, he lived at Farm Hill outside Belfast, but eventually settled at Glen Devis. He died on 25th June 1868. He had two sons and three daughters. Only one of his children survived him.

A relation of Mitchell who was involved in banking, had an entry off High Street named after him. It was originally called George Mitchell Entry and is now known as High Street Court.

JOHN JOSEPH ('RINTY') MONAGHAN *(1920–84)* | Flyweight boxer

Belfast is renowned for its boxers, and 'Rinty' Monaghan, also known as 'Rinty, the Pride of Belfast' and 'The Singing Irishman', was undoubtedly one of the best the city has produced. He was born in the docks area of North Belfast.

Monaghan became a professional boxer at the age of 14 and in 1945 won the Irish title by knockout against Bunty Doran. He won the World Flyweight title at Belfast's King's Hall on 23rd March 1948, when he knocked out Scot Jackie Patterson.

Rinty successfully defended his title in 1949 against Maurice Sanderson. The same year he drew with Terry Allen. He retired undefeated six months later. Of 54 professional fights, he won 43, drew three and lost eight. Monaghan held the British, European, Commonwealth and World titles simultaneously. Apparently, Rinty got his nickname from the film star dog Rin Tin Tin, because of his speedy footwork.

Monaghan was a friendly, genial man. He is famed for singing 'When Irish Eyes are Smiling' after every fight, and took to the cabaret circuit when he retired (but with little success). He also worked as a taxi and lorry driver and a garage attendant. He loved his

North Belfast neighbourhood and never wished to move. It is said he helped his neighbours financially rather than move upmarket himself.

Monaghan died at home on 3rd March, 1984 and was survived by his wife Frances, and six children.

BRIAN MOORE *(1921–99)* | Novelist

Brian Moore was undoubtedly one of the most important post-war Irish writers. He came to prominence in the mid-1950s and stayed in the vanguard of international literature for the rest of his life. Moore won many literary plaudits, including the Authors' Club First Novel Award for *The Lonely Passion of Judith Hearne*. He was short-listed for the Booker Prize on three occasions.

Born into a middle-class family in 1921 in Clifton Street, North Belfast, Moore was one of nine children and attended St Malachy's College on the Antrim Road. He went on to serve with the British Transport Division during the Second World War. He left Belfast in the 1940s and returned only sporadically. Much of his life was spent in America and Canada, where he worked as a journalist before turning to full-time fiction writing.

The Lonely Passion of Judith Hearne (1955) is set in South Belfast and charts the decline and fall of an alcoholic woman who clings to respectability, but finds a bottle or two of the hard stuff dulls the pain of failure and guilt. The novel brought Moore to the attention of the literary world. Here was a writer who could describe accurately how human beings relate to one another, whilst equally conveying the themes of poverty, religion and deprivation. The novel was made into a film in 1987 starring Maggie Smith.

Moore became renowned for writing about many different subjects with a rare ease and authority. His formative experiences hardened his dislike of Catholic discipline and rote. This is evident in several of his novels, but none so much as *Catholics* (1972) which won the W.H. Smith Award in 1973. This novella of tight, intense prose describes how an American papal nuncio is sent to deliver correction to a monastery off the West of Ireland, because it has used its peripheral geography to adopt a different interpretation of the faith.

Much of his work has an autobiographical feel. Moore joined the Air Raid Precaution Corps (ARP) when he left school, and in *The Emperor of Ice Cream* (1965) the central character takes the same path after missing out on a university place. Personal elements also appear in *An Answer from Limbo* (1962) and *The Luck of Ginger Coffey* (1960), set in America and Canada respectively.

Moore was short-listed for the Booker prize in 1976, for *The Doctor's Wife*, set on Belfast's Antrim Road. Apparently its racy material raised a few eyebrows in North Belfast when it was first published. *Lies of Silence* (1990) was also set in Belfast. It represented quite a departure for Moore. His first thriller, it explored the mentality of local terrorism. One of Moore's last pieces of writing, *The Statement* (1995), was another tense thriller. Speaking in 1996 during a visit to Belfast, Moore said, 'I like to keep changing my style. I find I never really know the format until I've started writing and once I start, I simply focus on one story at a time.'

Moore retained a passion for the local Arts, lending his weight to the Brian Moore Short Story Awards. The event started in the mid-1990s and is now an international competition organised by the Creative Writers' Network.

Moore married twice. He died in Malibu, California in 1999. In 1987 he had been awarded an honorary doctorate from Queen's University.

VAN MORRISON *(1945–)* | Singer

Arguably one of the most talented popular musicians of the late 20th century, George Ivan Morrison was born and grew up in Hyndford Street in the Beersbridge Road area of East Belfast. The son of a Harland & Wolff shipyard worker who collected American blues and jazz records, he grew up listening to the music of Muddy Waters, Mahalia Jackson, Lightnin' Hopkins and John Lee Hooker.

As a teenager he played guitar, sax and harmonica with a series of local showbands, skiffle and rock'n'roll groups, including the Monarchs, before forming an r&b band called Them in 1964. With Morrison as lead vocalist, Them had a popular residency at the Maritime Hotel in College Square North in Belfast.

In 1967, he began his solo career in New York where he recorded an LP titled *Blowin' Your Mind* with the producer Bert Berns. Following Berns' death in 1968 Morrison recruited a group of jazz musicians to record *Astral Weeks*, a classic album which brought together elements of Celtic music, improvised jazz and r&b.

Based in Boston and then California, Morrison produced a string of albums including *Moondance, Tupelo Honey* and *St Dominic's Preview,* while touring extensively with his band Caledonia Soul Orchestra. In 1974, he returned to Ireland, and his album *Veedon Fleece* featured a quieter, more pastoral sound. In 1977, the album *A Period of Transition* appeared, and after relocating to London, he released *Wavelength* in 1978 and *Into the Music* in 1979, by which time Morrison's interest in spiritual matters was finding regular expression in his recordings. The spiritual theme was evident in the albums of the 1980s: *Common One, Beautiful Vision, Inarticulate Speech of the Heart, A Sense of Wonder, No Guru No Method No Teacher* and *Poetic Champions Compose.*

In 1988 he revisited his roots with The Chieftains (Derek Bell is another accomplished Belfast-born musician) on *Irish Heartbeat.* In 1989 the album *Avalon Sunset* was a huge

Van Morrison at the Belfast Festival at Queen's

commercial success, and in the 1990s Morrison varied his musical approach. *Enlightenment* (1990), and *Hymns to the Silence* (1991) continued along the road to spiritual self-discovery, while *Too Long in Exile* (1993) leaned towards the blues. After *Days Like This* (1995) came *How Long Has This Been Going On* (1995), an album of jazz standards featuring his old sparring partner Georgie Fame. Following *The Healing Game* (1997) and *The Philosopher's Stone* (1998), Morrison won a Grammy for his collaboration with John Lee Hooker on *Don't Look Back*, which he also produced. In 1999 *Back On Top* was released, spawning his first Top 40 hit single 'Precious Time'.

In 2000 Morrison's musical career came full-circle with *The Skiffle Sessions – Live in Belfast*. Re-uniting with the heroes of his youth, he joined skiffle maestro Lonnie Donegan and Chris Barber at the Whitla Hall at Queen's University.

Morrison has never aimed to be a crowd-pleaser, preferring to be known through his music alone. He was awarded an honorary doctorate by Queen's in 2001.

ANDREW MULHOLLAND *(1790–1866)* | Industrialist

Around 1815, the Mulholland brothers, Thomas (1786–1830), Andrew (1790–1866) and St Clair (1798–1872) purchased cotton mills when the cotton industry was flourishing. They purchased McCammond, Milford and Bailey's mill in Winetavern Street in 1815 and acquired another, McCracken's old mill, in Francis Street. In 1822 they built a further mill in Henry Street.

Industry was changing, however. The cotton spinning industry peaked around 1825, and locally the trade was hindered when the tariff barrier protecting Irish cotton was lifted in 1824. In 1828 the Mulholland's Henry Street mill burned down. Ironically, this disaster proved fortuitous.

Before rebuilding the mill, the Mulhollands looked into the possibility of spinning flax rather than cotton. The brothers and their Mancunian partner John Hind went to Leeds, York and Lancaster on a fact-finding mission and specifically to look into James Kay's (unpatented) process of wet-spinning flax. The Mulhollands experimented by establishing 1,000 flax spinners in the Francis Street mill. This proved a great success, and the new York Street mill, built in 1830, with 8,000 spindles, became one of the biggest linen mills of its kind in the world. It was so successful that it resulted in a rush amongst cotton spinners to adapt their mills for spinning flax. The mill also proved extremely profitable, making Andrew Mulholland one of Belfast's richest entrepreneurs – Thomas had died in 1830 and St Clair had gone into business separately with Hind, forming S.K. Mulholland & Hind (later John Hind & Co.) of Durham Street.

Andrew Mulholland married Elizabeth McDonnell in 1818, and they had one son and four daughters. He was elected Lord Mayor of Belfast in 1845, promising to better conditions by providing public gardens, wash-houses, free libraries and coffee shops. Famine, however, thwarted his plans for improvement, although he contributed generously to famine relief. In 1862, Mulholland provided Belfast's civic hall, the Ulster Hall, with a magnificent grand organ, which is still the pride of the venue today.

The family moved to Ballywalter Park, Co. Down (the house was designed by Sir Charles Lanyon) in 1846. They had previously lived in York Street, then later at Mount Collyer. Andrew Mulholland was later assisted in business by his son John and the firm became Andrew Mulholland & Son. John Mulholland, who had been the M.P. for Downpatrick, became the first Lord Dunleath in 1892.

ROGER MULHOLLAND *(1740–1818)* | Architect

Roger Mulholland was Belfast's most important architect of the late 18th century. Born in Co. Derry/Londonderry in 1740, Mulholland moved to Belfast and lived at 12 Castle Street. Initially a carpenter, he was involved in many projects organised by the fifth Earl of Donegall.

Donegall made several sites available to Mulholland, who supervised building in Academy Street, Talbot Street and Donegall Street. The jewel in his crown was the First Presbyterian Church in Rosemary Street (1781–3). He also supervised work on St Anne's Church built in 1776 (later demolished to make way, in 1898, for St Anne's Cathedral, to designs by Thomas Drew), which had a distinctive columned portico and tall domed tower, and the Belfast Assembly Rooms.

Mulholland took a lease in 1789 on a timber yard near Ann Street and he continued his building work in Hill Street and Dunbar Street. He married Jane Russell in 1770 and in 1780 they moved to Cromac Lodge, then on the outskirts of town close to the Ormeau Road, where he built some of the first houses in the area.

Roger Mulholland had a connection, as an investor, with the White Linen Hall, built in 1783 where the City Hall now stands. He was also responsible for the building of the former coach house on the site of Belfast Castle, and was involved in constructing three three-storey houses fronting Donegall Place. One of these houses, number 25, still stands and is the only remaining 18th-century house in Donegall Place. It went from being a private residence in the 19th century to a fur house, Lowry & Co., to the Carlton Café in the inter-war years, replete with a stained glass canopy in front. It is now occupied by the retail shop Oasis. Later Mulholland commissions included the House of Correction at the corner of Howard Street, which was the town gaol at the time.

Mulholland moved back to Castle Street in 1809. He died on 30th November 1818, leaving over £3,500 to his children, George, Margaret, Mary and Cunningham. Also a founder of the Linen Hall Library, he was an important figure in Belfast's urban development.

SIR JAMES MURRAY *(1788–1871)* | Doctor and Inventor of Milk of Magnesia

James Murray was an apothecary whose most notable contribution to medicine was the invention of that most revered and reviled of liquid remedies, Milk of Magnesia.

Born in 1788, he was appointed in 1807, aged only 19, as the apothecary of Belfast's Dispensary and Fever Hospital (later the Royal Victoria Hospital, see JAMES McDONNELL). He resigned a year later to set up as a surgeon and apothecary in High Street.

In 1829, he used his fluid magnesia preparation to settle a stomach illness that was ailing the Marquess of Anglesey, Lord Lieutenant of Ireland, who was in Belfast visiting the Marquess of Donegall. The treatment was so successful that Murray was appointed resident Physician to the Lord Lieutenant.

In 1828 he was involved in building a fine range of large houses in Belfast, known as Murray's Terrace, which gave their name to present-day Murray Street.

Knighted for his services to the Lord Lieutenant, Murray was awarded MD of Edinburgh University in 1829 and obtained an MD from Trinity College, Dublin in 1832. He died in 1871 and is buried in Clifton Street Graveyard.

Murray's magnesia preparation was later patented by Charles H. Phillips in 1873 and subsequently sold as Milk of Magnesia.

RUBY MURRAY *(1935–96)* | Singer

In 1954, Ruby Murray, a 19-year-old girl from the Donegall Road, topped the UK singles charts with the ballad 'Softly, softly'. In all she had five records in the top ten at the same time – a record that she now shares with The Beatles.

Murray was born off Broadway and the family then moved to Benburb Street. She loved singing from an early age, starting in her Presbyterian church choir (which she was later told to leave because of her stage role). Her father was involved in putting on shows in church halls and at the Ulster Hall. As a teenager she was soon topping these bills. Leaving school at 14, Ruby took a series of jobs, but soon realised her real talents lay in show-business. Rave reviews led her to the attention of the Delfont Agency, which auditioned and signed her up.

At the time of 'Softly, softly', she was living with her uncle in London, using the house as a base for tours. When asked at the time how she listened to her songs, she replied 'on the wireless!' – there was no record player at her uncle's home. She was signed for £100 a week – good money in 1955 but hardly commensurate with her star status.

In November 1955, *New Musical Express* readers voted her their favourite female artiste, ahead of the established favourite Alma Cogan. Murray topped the bill at the Palladium that year and she was among the first stars to benefit from television. Musicals, work abroad with The Combined Services Entertainment, and even a role as an Irish chambermaid in *A Touch of the Sun* with Frankie Howerd, soon broadened her experience. There was a downside, how-

Ruby Murray

ever. Despite much effort on her part, her show-business marriage failed. Money worries and heavy drinking also took their toll.

Ruby Murray remarried in the early 1990s (to her original sweetheart) and lived happily in Torquay, Devon. Sadly, health problems resurfaced and she died of liver cancer in December 1996 after being ill for some time. In 2001, MARIE JONES wrote and produced a tribute to the singer, *Ruby*, which was performed in the Group Theatre. Ruby's name has also now passed into Cockney rhyming slang immortality – to go for 'a Ruby Murray' is to go out for a curry!

PATRICK NEILL (d.1705) and JAMES BLOW (d.1759) | Printers

Although there may have been some presses in Belfast by the 1690s to satisfy the needs of an educated public, Patrick Neill was the first established printer in the town. He and James Blow, his brother-in-law, printed the New Testament sometime between 1694 and 1705 (no copy is known to survive).

Belfast's Sovereign, William Crawford, invited Neill to Belfast from Glasgow in 1694, and he soon settled, and started printing pamphlets and sermons. He brought Blow with him, and Blow took over the business when Neill died in 1705.

The business continued to thrive under James Blow. In the early 18th century, along with a George Grierson, Blow printed the Bible; the first printer to do so in Ireland. Blow also produced the *Church Catechism in Irish* in 1722 'with the English placed over it in the same karakter'. His printing of the Bible and his other religious output wasn't appreciated by everyone – the Vicar of Belfast (1704–36), Doctor William Tisdall, who was an intolerant High and anti-Presbyterian Churchman, unsuccessfully tried to censor much of Blow's religious material.

Blow also published an edition of works of the well-known 16th-century Scottish poet and satirist Sir David Lindsay. By 1747 he was in partnership with his son Daniel, to whom he left his estate. Blow lived until 1759, by which time other printers, including FRANCIS JOY, were well established.

(JOHN) HAVELOCK NELSON (1917–96) | Musician

Born in Cork in 1917, Havelock Nelson became one of the most influential people in the Belfast classical music field. He studied Music and Science and went on to blend the two careers. Nelson lectured in Microbiology at Trinity College, Dublin and was also one of that city's most prominent musicians.

Nelson co-founded the Dublin Orchestral Players before going to work in Belfast where he became an accompanist with the BBC. He also worked as a conductor and recitalist and founded the Studio Opera Group in the 1960s. Working tirelessly and creatively for local music, becoming Director of the Ulster Singers in 1974; at the same time, he adjudicated at festivals throughout the world. In 1976 he founded the Trinidad and Tobago Opera company. Four of his nine doctorates were in recognition of his services to the arts in Jamaica, Trinidad and Barbados. Nelson was awarded the O.B.E. for Services to Music in 1966.

Nelson's work did much to shape musical direction in Northern Ireland. The Castleward Opera developed from his Studio Opera Group. He contributed greatly to the Belfast Festival at Queen's, conducting at many of its events. He also made many choral and vocal arrangements of Irish folk music.

Havelock Nelson died in Belfast on 5th August 1996. He is survived by two sons and one daughter.

ANDREW NICHOLL *(1804–86)* | Artist

Andrew Nicholl was one of Ireland's leading 19th-century watercolourists and landscape artists. He was born on 4th April 1804 in Church Lane, where his father had his boot-making premises. He worked with F.D. Finlay, printers, and gave drawing lessons in his spare time. Nicholl's early paintings were often to be found in the windows of William McComb's stationery and bookshop in Cornmarket.

In 1824, Finlay started *The Northern Whig* newspaper. Nicholl worked with him, mainly as an illustrator. He was, however, painting all the time outside work, and before 1830 had completed a comprehensive series of watercolours of the Antrim Coast. In 1830, Nicholl crossed to London, working there for two years before going to Dublin, where the *Dublin Penny Journal* carried illustrations from his drawings. He also supplied 13 pictures for Robert Clayton's engravings for *Views of the Dublin and Kingstown Railway* in 1835.

More commissions followed, and between 1836 and 1838, he exhibited annually with the Belfast Association of Artists. Andrew's brother, William, also exhibited. William's landscape work was well respected.

In 1837, Nicholl became an Associate of the Royal Hibernian Academy, and he also contributed to the Royal Academy in London until 1854. He illustrated *Hall's Ireland* with scenic paintings in the early 1840s. In 1840 he went to London to both paint and teach, and the Government appointed him teacher of Painting and Drawing at Colombo Academy.

In 1840, he carried out much commissioned scenic work throughout Ireland including 12 lithographs *The Northern Coast of Ireland*. From 1850 onwards Nicholl divided his time between London, Dublin and Belfast, basing himself at 27 College Street whilst in Belfast. In 1846 he visited Ceylon, where his friend, another Belfast man, Sir James Emerson Tennant, was Colonial Secretary.

He died on April 16th 1886, at 7 Camberwell Grove, London. An exhibition of his work followed in May at 55 Donegall Place. His paintings are on display at the Ulster Museum, in the National Library of Ireland, the Linen Hall Library and in the Victoria and Albert Museum and the British Museum.

CATHAL O'BYRNE *(1874–1957)* | Folklorist

Born in 1874 in Co. Down, Cathal O'Byrne was known as 'The Prince of Storytellers'. A folklorist, author and dramatist, he worked in business in Belfast for a time, before switching careers to go touring around Ireland and Britain, singing and giving recitals as he went.

O'Byrne wrote a column called 'Mrs Twigglety' in *Ireland's Saturday Night*, and he also wrote verse, mainly of a rhythmical, rhyming variety, as well as some plays.

A storyteller in the old tradition, he is best remembered for *As I Roved Out*, a set of historical, rambling stories about Belfast and beyond. The collection was first published in 1946, but began as an extensive series of 'historical sketches of Ulster and Old Belfast' in the *Irish News*. The book was dedicated to his friend FRANCIS JOSEPH BIGGER.

O'Byrne was active in the Gaelic League and in the 1920s went to America on behalf of the White Cross Fund for those who had suffered in the Troubles of 1921–2. He was renowned for his physical appearance; flushed red face, black hair, and an enormous ring on the little finger of his left hand.

Cathal O'Byrne died on August 2nd, 1957, aged 83. *As I Roved Out* was re-published after his death and a foreword by JOHN HEWITT was included in the 1982 edition.

FRANK PANTRIDGE *(1916–)* | Cardiologist

Innovative and unorthodox, Professor James Francis Pantridge has been lauded for his revolutionary defibrillator that since 1965 has saved thousands of lives.

Born near Hillsborough, Pantridge attended Downshire and Friend's Schools before commencing the study of Medicine at Queen's in 1934. (One of his teachers was Thompson Flynn, Professor of Zoology and father to Errol Flynn). He graduated as M.B. in 1939.

At the outbreak of the Second World War, Pantridge volunteered and was sent to the Far East as Medical Officer to an infantry battalion. He was captured in 1942 with the fall of Singapore. He won a Military Cross for his services in the appalling conditions in Malaya. His tenacity was also evident in surviving Tanbaya, the Burmese death camp.

After the War, in 1946, Pantridge returned to Belfast to complete his houseman's year, and then worked as a general physician in the Royal Victoria Hospital, focusing on Cardiology. He worked on the development of pre-

Professor James Francis Pantridge, Consultant Cardiologist, Royal Victoria Hospital, 1951–82

hospital coronary care, revolutionising emergency medicine. He wasn't afraid of flouting convention, and investigated cardiac beriberi by bringing pigs into the hospital laboratory.

In 1951, he was appointed Consultant Physician to Outpatients and established the Cardiac Department at the Royal. Twenty years later, the Department had 80 patients and Pantridge had established the Regional Medical Cardiology Centre. He had realised fatal heart attacks usually occurred away from hospital, out of reach of medical attention.

In 1965, he and Dr John Geddes produced a portable defibrillator; a machine capable of delivering an electric shock to the arrested heart and resetting the rhythm. He also pioneered the world's first cardiac ambulance. The Belfast Mobile Coronary Care Unit was initially criticised in the UK, but the defibrillator's success was immediate in America, where Pantridge was often asked to speak. Pantridge's innovations silenced the critics. Results spoke for themselves. He has always been dismissive of his worldwide reputation and stressed the simplicity of his invention. He was awarded the C.B.E. in 1979, and retired in 1982. His autobiography, *An Unquiet Life*, was published in 1989.

STEWART PARKER *(1941–88)* | Playwright

Stewart Parker's writing career was tragically cut short at the age of 47. He left a fine legacy of award-winning productions for both stage and screen.

Parker was born in Sydenham on 20th October 1941. He went to Ashfield Intermediate School and later studied English at Queen's. Aged 19, he contracted bone cancer and had to have a leg amputated. After taking an M.A. specialising in Poetic Drama in 1966, he taught in

America at Hamilton College and Cornell University. In the meantime, Parker had married Kate Ireland, and become involved with a group of writers including BERNARD MACLAVERTY and Seamus Heaney. In 1968, Parker returned to Belfast as a freelancer, where his work included writing for radio. He wrote a column for the *Irish Times* between 1971 and 1976.

His first television play *Private Grounds* was produced in 1975. From there, his career gained momentum. *Spokesong*, a comedy set in Belfast, saw Parker win the *Evening Standard* award for Most Promising Playwright. First staged at the Dublin Theatre Festival, it later played in the West End. In 1978, his success took him first to Edinburgh and then to London. His television play *Montreal* won the Christopher Ewart-Biggs Memorial Prize, and six of his works were broadcast on ITV and Channel 4 as *Lost Belongings*.

In the 1980s, Parker produced a trilogy of history plays: *Northern Star*, *Heavenly Bodies* and *Pentecost*, which was set in May 1974 during the Ulster Workers' strike. The theme is the need for love and reconciliation. Staged by Field Day Theatre Company, it was a fitting end to Parker's short but brilliant career. He died of cancer in London on 2nd November 1988.

GLENN PATTERSON *(1961–)* | Novelist

Glenn Patterson, who was born and lives in Belfast, is an established novelist, having published four acclaimed works, all based to a greater or lesser extent around local life.

He was educated at Methodist College, Belfast, from 1973 to 1980, and worked in a Belfast bookshop before studying Creative Writing at the Univeristy of East Anglia. He subsequently became a Writer in the Community in both Lisburn and Craigavon from 1989 to 1991 and a Creative Writing Fellow at the University of East Anglia in 1992, Writer in Residency at University College, Cork, and Writer in Residence at Queen's University from 1994 to 1997.

His first novel *Burning Your Own* (1988) won the Rooney Prize for Irish Literature and a Betty Trask Prize. Set during the summer of 1969, the novel is about the reaction of a group of boys on a Belfast housing estate to the developing political tension.

Glenn Patterson

Fat Lad, written in 1992, is set in Belfast in 1990, as an element of regeneration starts to become evident in the city. The main character, Drew, is a young man drawn back to Belfast by a new job. Patterson uses flashbacks to explain tension between Drew and his father, and depicts their family history in a way that also encompasses the Troubles. *Fat Lad* displays symbolism about the newness of nineties Belfast blended with the backdrop of a troubled city and its industrial past. *Fat Lad* was short-listed for the GPA Book award.

Patterson has written two further novels, *Black Night at Big Thunder Mountain* (1995) and *The International* (1999), about a day in the life of the Belfast hotel of the same name in 1967. The story, seen mainly through the eyes of 18-year-old barman Danny, is set just as political tensions were beginning to manifest in Belfast. The novel presents Danny's perspective on the lives of the patrons, and captures a tight, aggressive form of Belfast banter and wit. A fifth novel, *No. 5*, is due for publication in 2002.

TOM PAULIN *(1949–)* | Poet and critic

A familiar face – and Belfast voice – on BBC's television arts programme *Newsnight Review*, Tom Paulin is an acclaimed poet and critic.

Born in Leeds in 1949, Paulin grew up in Belfast in North Parade off the Ormeau Road. He read English at Hull University and continued his studies at Oxford. His volumes of poetry include *Walking a Line*, which was short-listed for the T.S. Eliot Prize in 1994; *The Wind Dog*; and *Fivemiletown,* which focuses on the local conflict. Paulin also acts as a drama critic and has written a critique of Thomas Hardy's poetry, and of William Hazlitt's prose.

Paulin, who has received several other poetry awards, is also a playwright – *The Hillsborough Script* is a political satire – and was a Director of the Field Day Theatre Company. He was Professor of Poetry at Nottingham University, before being appointed G.M. Young Lecturer in English Literature at Hertford College, Oxford.

MARY PETERS *(1939–)* | Athlete

Northern Ireland's only Olympic Gold Medallist is Mary Peters, whose smiling face has graced sports media coverage internationally. She has worked tirelessly for both local charities and athletics, and is steeped in local life.

Dame Mary Peters with her Olympic Gold Medal

Work brought her father to Northern Ireland from Lancashire in the early 1950s. When the family came across, they moved first to Ballymena and then to Portadown where 11-year-old Mary started to show athletic talent at Portadown College. The shot-put was her main event, and her father drove her all over Ulster to compete.

In 1958, she began studying at Belfast's Domestic Economy Training College. Now a pentathlete, she finished second in the 1956 British Pentathlon Championships and went on to compete in the Cardiff Commonwealth Games. In 1960, she passed her exams and started teaching Domestic Science at Graymount Girl's Secondary

School in North Belfast. She also met Robert 'Buster' McShane, weight-lifting coach to the Northern Ireland team. She started to train at his gym and Buster became her coach.

Peters initially worked part time at Buster's gym, but as the business grew, gave up teaching and worked there full time, giving her the opportunity to devote more time to training. In 1961, she was selected for her first UK team and finished fifth in the European Championships. In 1964, she took fourth place at the Tokyo Olympic Games, was made captain of the British women's team in 1965, and in 1966 achieved Silver in the shot-put in the Commonwealth Games.

She started the 1970s in terrific form, equalling the indoor 60 metre hurdles world record. At Edinburgh a new points record secured a Commonwealth Gold in the pentathlon, and she also won the shot-put. In 1971, she secured a scholarship grant to help her train for the 1972 Munich Olympics, which she saw as her last realistic opportunity for Olympic Gold.

'Mary P.' was quite fancied for the Gold, but with the two German athletes Rosendahl and Pollak in the running, could take nothing for granted. At the end of the first day's events, Mary was in the lead. A good performance in the long jump meant she just had to stay in reach of Rosendahl in the 200 metres – and she did. Before the victory had sunk in, the celebrations began. The *Belfast Telegraph* organised a welcome home party – and started the Mary Peters track fund – and she was soon whisked off on a celebrity circuit that included *This is Your Life*, the *Daily Express* Sportswoman of the Year Award and BBC Sports Personality of the Year.

Buster McShane's death in 1973 saddened her terribly, but she immersed herself in work at the club and in a campaign to improve the Queen's track at Upper Malone in Belfast, which was renamed in her honour. Inspired by Mary's attitude and work, the *Belfast Telegraph* and the Education Ministry were both major contributors towards the achievement.

In 1974 Peters retired after taking Gold in the Pentathlon at the Commonwealth Games in New Zealand. She later gave up McShane's, and became a member of the Sports Council, the Northern Ireland BBC's Advisory Council, the Northern Ireland Tourist Board, and kept active with other charities. She also went on to open a health studio in Lisburn. Peters was awarded an M.B.E. in 1973, a C.B.E. in 1990 and was made a Dame in 2000.

WILLIAM JAMES PIRRIE *(1847–1924)* | Chairman of Harland & Wolff

Pirrie was the driving force of his time behind Harland & Wolff. Under his energetic control, the business expanded tenfold as new methods of design enabled the Yard to produce huge and innovative ships such as the *Titanic*. Born in Quebec on 24th May 1847 of a Co. Down family, Pirrie was educated at the Royal Belfast Academical Institution and became an apprentice gentleman at Queen's Island as Harland & Wolff was establishing its reputation. Pirrie learned quickly, and armed with an aptitude for engineering, drive and charm, he was made a partner in 1874.

In 1879 he married his cousin, Margaret Montgomery Carlisle. She took a great interest in the business, and was to prove a useful ally for her husband. A newly developed triple expansion engine gave the shipyard a boost, together with links with the White Star Liverpool liners that led to ships like the *Teutonic* being built. The *Teutonic* on its maiden voyage crossed the Atlantic in a record six days 17 hours and 25 minutes.

With Pirrie as Chairman, the shipyard boomed. He became Lord Mayor in 1896, and a Privy Councillor the following year. His new designs were a great success. The *Briton* was the largest liner not on a transatlantic run. The *Oceanic* was the largest ship of its time. With the *Laurentic* came new and complex methods of building and fitting marine turbines.

Portrait of William Pirrie, Chairman of Harland & Wolff, Lord Mayor of Belfast

Pirrie could be dictatorial. His brother-in-law, A. M. Carlisle resigned in 1911, and although no reason was given, personality differences undoubtedly played a part. On 14th April 1912 came the terrible shock of the *Titanic*'s sinking and, of course, the death of his designer Thomas Andrews. It took Pirrie time to recover from this awful blow.

After 1918, Pirrie made radical preparations for future design and construction against a backdrop of Trade Union unrest. He managed to keep morale high by organizing sports fixtures at a new ground named Pirrie Park off Ardenlee Avenue in South Belfast (now the Methodist College playing fields and site of Downey House Preparatory School). He became a member of the new Northern Ireland Senate and was granted a peerage in 1922.

In 1924, Pirrie was on board the *Arlanza* in Panama when he became ill. He declined rapidly and died on 7th June 1924, aged 77. When Lord Kylsant succeeded him at Harland & Wolff, it took time to rebuild the momentum. Lady Pirrie was appointed President of the company for life.

SIR HENRY POTTINGER *(1789–1856)* | First Governor of Hong Kong

One of the fascinating aspects of a city is the naming of streets and areas. Mount Pottinger, near the Templemore and Woodstock areas of East Belfast, is named after Sir Henry Pottinger, who lived at an address in the Mount, an attractive part of the area. However, much of Pottinger's colourful life was conducted abroad. The family's name is also asscociated with Pottinger's Entry and Pottinger's Court, off the lower part of High Street.

He was born in 1789, the son of a radical who formed the Volunteer Corp in 1779, but Henry was only ever partially involved in politics. Educated at Belfast Academy, he was sent to India as the family fortunes declined. Showing an early interest in travel, he became a midshipman in the Royal Navy in 1801. In 1806 he transferred to the East India Company army as an ensign. In 1809, he became Lieutenant of the Infantry and fought in the Maliratta War.

Whilst in Asia, he explored much of the land between Indus and Persia, and is said to have travelled in disguise as a Mohammedan merchant. In 1820, he was appointed Resident Administrator of Sind, and later Hyderabad. He was promoted to Colonel and later became Chief Superintendent of Trade. Pottinger returned to England as a baronet, but in 1842 his experience in the East again proved invaluable when he negotiated the Treaty of Nanking which ended the first Opium War.

Pottinger also acquired, against orders, Hong Kong as a British Crown Colony as part of the deal. Later, he was appointed its first Governor. Further appointments followed, including Grand Commander of the Order of the Bath. In 1847, he became Governor of Madras and in 1851, Lieutenant General.

Pottinger retired to Malta, where he died in 1856. Married to Susanna Maria Cooke of Cookesborough, Westmeath, he had three sons and one daughter. A memorial plaque was erected to him by his brother in St George's Church in High Street, and an Ulster History Circle plaque marks the spot of The Mount in Mount Pottinger.

FORREST REID *(1875–1952)* | Novelist

Those who live in East Belfast may be familiar with the plaque to Forrest Reid placed on the wall of 13 Ormiston Crescent. Reid was arguably Belfast's first widely recognised novelist. Born at 20 Mount Charles, Belfast in 1875, he attended the Royal Belfast Academical Institution before studying Mediaeval and Modern Languages at Christ's College, Cambridge.

After graduating, Reid returned to Belfast where he spent the rest of his life in an atmosphere of fading gentility. He made his name with the acclaimed novels *The Retreat* (1936), *Peter Waring* (1937) – regarded by some as his best work – and *Young Tom* (1944).

Popular throughout the British Isles, his books also sold well on the Continent.

Reid also published literary criticism, including books on W.B. Yeats and Walter de la Mare, a children's writer and illustrator. Both men were longstanding friends. Reid was also very friendly with the highly-regarded novelist Henry James, but they fell out when Reid dedicated his book *The Garden God* to him – James is said to have been embarrassed by its homosexual undertones.

Portrait of Forrest Reid by James Sinton Slator (1924), Ulster Museum

Reid's writing talents were diverse. He wrote articles for magazines, including *The Westminster Review* and *The Ulster Review*, and also published *Illustrators of the Sixties*, a study of Victorian woodcut artists. He was also involved in occasional radio broadcasting.

A founder member of the Irish Academy of Letters, Reid published his autobiography *Apostate* in 1926. *Private Road*, its sequel, followed in 1940. He died on 4th January 1947 and is buried in Dundonald Cemetery. The plaque to him was unveiled five years after his death on 10th October 1952. Both E. M. Forster and Walter de la Mare addressed the gathering.

WILLIAM RITCHIE *(1755–1834)* | Shipbuilder

Born in Saltcoats, Ayrshire, William Ritchie and his brothers developed early shipbuilding in Belfast. He visited Belfast with the aim of establishing a shipyard, which he did on the site of the Old Lime Kiln Dock, just north of the present Waring Street.

Ritchie wasted no time and on 7th July 1792 the 300 ton *Hibernia* was launched, the largest vessel of its time to be built in Belfast . By 1795 he had set up a dry dock, and the yard continued to prosper. He was also employed by the Ballast Board to build its first dock which was completed in 1800.

Ritchie brought ship joiners, block makers and blacksmiths over from Scotland, and by 1811, had built 31 ships of up to 450 tons. His brothers Hugh and John both had yards in Belfast (they had been partners with William until 1798).

Ritchie retired in the 1820s, leaving the business

Portrait of William Ritchie, attributed to Thomas Robinson, Belfast Harbour Office

in the safe hands of his Scottish assistant Charles Connell. Ritchie, who was also involved in charitable work for the Poor House (Clifton House) in North Queen Street, died in 1834, aged 78. Ritchie's efforts provided a launching pad for the work of HARLAND, WOLFF and PIRRIE.

CHARLES RUSSELL, BARON RUSSELL OF KILLOWEN *(1832–1900)* | British Lord Chief Justice

Born in Newry but educated in Belfast, Charles Russell became a successful lawyer in London. Elevated to Lord of Appeal in 1894, he was appointed Lord Chief Justice very soon afterwards; the first Catholic to attain the position since the Reformation.

Russell was from a middle class background. He was educated firstly at Harkin's School in Castle Street, Belfast and then at St Malachy's College on the Antrim Road. His final years of schooling were at Castleknock in Dublin. Russell qualified as a solicitor and practised for two years in Belfast. He built up a reputation as a lawyer who would stoutly defend the Catholic cause, particularly during these early years of unrest in Belfast's history.

Russell's fiancée, Ellen Mulholland, encouraged him to go to the Bar. Russell was known for his clear head and strong will, traits also shared by Ellen. The couple married in August 1858 at St Malachy's Church, Alfred Street, Belfast. His mother-in-law presented him with £1,000 and this capital helped him start at the Bar in 1859. He proved a great success, taking silk in 1872.

Russell became involved in politics. He was Independent Liberal MP for Dundalk in 1880, and represented South Hackney from 1885 until 1894; he supported the Irish Party's Home Rule policy.

Attorney General in Gladstone's administrations of 1886 and 1892, Russell was cross-examiner in the famous Parnell trial, where he destroyed the evidence of Pigott, the author of the forged letters.

In the 1890s, Russell received many of his plaudits. He was awarded the Grand Order of St Michael and St George in 1893 for his part in the Bering Sea Arbitration. Lord of Appeal in 1894, he was then created Baron Russell of Killowen. Although he only held the position of Lord Chief Justice for a few years, he is said to have won the public's confidence.

Russell died after a brief illness in London. He was survived by Ellen and his nine children.

BETTY SINCLAIR *(1900–71)* | Trade Unionist and Politician

Betty Sinclair was a founding member of the Communist Party of Ireland, Secretary of the Belfast Trades Council and a member of the Northern Ireland Civil Rights Association. Born in 1900 into a Labour orientated Protestant family in Castlereagh, Sinclair lived nearly all her life in Belfast. She worked in Jennymount Linen Mill and, interested in Trade Unions, joined the Workers Revolutionary Group in 1929.

Sinclair was on the first Central Committee after the inception of the Communist Party of Ireland in 1933. She represented the Party at many international congresses and worked briefly in Prague and Moscow. She remained active during the Second World War, and was sentenced to two months' imprisonment for distributing seditious literature in 1940. In 1945, she unsuccessfully contested the Cromac seat in Belfast. In 1947, she was elected Secretary of the Belfast Trades Council. She carried out trade union business and ran a Citizen's Advice Bureau in her office, helping people regardless of religion or position.

When the Northern Ireland Civil Rights Association formed in May 1965, Sinclair became Chairperson. She represented the Belfast Trades Council on the Northern Ireland Committee of the Irish Congress of Trade Unions.

Known as kindly yet businesslike, Sinclair was a popular political figure. She died at her home in Cregagh on 24th December 1971 and was buried at Carnmoney Cemetery.

THOMAS SINCLAIR *(1838–1914)* | Businessman and Philanthropist

The Right Honourable Thomas Sinclair was a man of many interests and talents. Born in Fisherwick Place on 23rd September 1838, he attended the Royal Belfast Academical Institution and Queen's College. Academically gifted, he achieved a B.A. at 18, together with a Gold Medal. In 1859, he attained an M.A. in English Literature.

Sinclair joined his father and brother in the family merchandise concern, J. and T. Sinclair. He worked hard but found time to be President of the Chamber of Commerce; he was also a member of the Barbour Trust. Sinclair helped establish the Royal Victoria Hospital and campaigned for better equipment at Queen's, although he declined a place on the Senate.

As a young man he became involved with the Presbyterian Church. He helped with a mission in Hardinge Street, and in 1859 worked with his father to establish Duncairn Church.

In 1861 he succeeded his father as Superintendent of Duncairn Sabbath School. Sinclair lobbied the General Assembly over the sustenation fund, to assist needy parishioners. He also took a lively interest in the church in Fisherwick Place, and in the Seaman's Friend Society; he was responsible, with the rest of his family, for the building of Sinclair Seamen's Church in Corporation Square (designed by SIR CHARLES LANYON) as a memorial to his father.

Sinclair was also concerned with the Land Question. Wanting to help local farmers, he was in favour of land reform in the 1880s. He saw himself as a 'Liberal of the Old School' but turned more towards Unionism as the Home Rule issue loomed.

Sinclair was a founding member of the Ulster Reform Club in Royal Avenue and was founder and first President of the Ulster Liberal Unionist Association. A polished orator, he was still making deputations to Asquith in his seventies. A keen cyclist in his youth, Sinclair also introduced golf to the north of Ireland. He helped form a golf club on the Kinnegar, and was Captain between 1881 and 1883.

Sinclair's first wife Mary died before him, but his second wife Elizabeth survived him. He had four sons and three daughters. He died in his home, Hopefield House, on the Antrim Road in 1914.

SISTER GENEVIEVE *(1923–2001)* | Educationalist

Sister Genevieve was one of the most important 20th-century figures in Belfast education. Against huge odds, she built St Louise's Comprehensive on the Falls Road into a successful school of 2,400 female pupils; few leaving without qualifications.

Born Mary O'Farrell on March 22nd 1923 in Tullamore, Co. Offaly, she joined the Daughters of Charity of St Vincent De Paul, and took a teacher training course in 1947. After teaching in Lanark near Glasgow until 1956, she moved to Belfast to teach in St Vincent's primary school on the Falls Road before helping to launch St Louise's on 8th January 1958.

Sister Genevieve assumed the role of headmistress in 1963. From the outset she insisted on discipline and control over unruly pupils, getting senior girls on her side and singling out troublemakers. She also made it plain she intended to educate everyone. Sister Genevieve put considerable emphasis on pupils getting qualifications, as she was determined that girls should get good jobs when they left. Gradually, St Louise's pupils took fewer and fewer unskilled jobs, helped both by their education and Sister Genevieve's job networking.

She didn't always see eye to eye with the clergy, the education boards or local

Sister Genevieve in her office at St Louise's school

people, but confrontation seemed to drive her on even more. When the Troubles started, Sister Genevieve faced up to this enormous challenge, for example refusing to shut the school during the hunger strike funerals. Sister Genevieve insisted on an air of normality in the school, however bad the trouble on the Falls became. The school was to be a haven.

She built up good working relations with ministers like Nicholas Scott, Rhodes Boyson and Brian Mawhinney. As the school got larger, she became an expert in delegation, working through her administration team. In her last year, St Louise's won a UK-wide award for educational achievement. Sister Genevieve retired as Principal in 1988. She had been awarded honorary degrees by Queen's and the University of Ulster. She was awarded an O.B.E. in 1976.

Between 1988 and 1994 she was an active prison visitor, helping both Catholic and Protestant terrorists in the Maze, encouraging them to study. Many went on to obtain first class degrees from the Open University. In 1994, Sister Genevieve suffered a severe stroke, and she died at her home in Belfast in December 2001.

WILLIAM THOMSON, LORD KELVIN *(1824–1907)*

Ground-breaking Physicist

Strolling through Botanic Gardens, it is hard to miss the imposing commemorative statue to William Thomson, who was one of the most important 19th-century British scientists. He was born on the 26th of June 1824 at College Square East on a site that later became the

The unveiling of the statue of Lord Kelvin (William Thomson), Botanic Gardens

home of Belfast's first cinema, appropriately called The Kelvin. His father, James, was Professor of Mathematics at the Belfast Academical Institution. The family moved in 1832, when James Thomson was appointed Professor of Mathematics at Glasgow University.

William commenced study, aged 11, at Glasgow University and continued his education at Peterhouse College, Cambridge, graduating in 1845. Glasgow University appointed him Professor of Natural Philosophy aged 22 in 1846, a position he held until 1899 when he retired, aged 75. In Glasgow, he carried out pioneering work on mechanical energy and heat. His work has become the basis of modern low-temperature engineering. The 'absolute' scale of temperature is named after him – on this scale the freezing point of water is 273.15 degrees Kelvin.

Thomson is also famous for inventing a sensitive mirror galvanometer, used in the first transatlantic telegraph cable of 1866. The cable ran from Valentia Island off Co. Kerry to Trinity Bay, Newfoundland. Thomson himself was aboard *The Great Eastern* which laid the cable.

Thomson was knighted for his work in 1866, and was created a peer, Baron Kelvin of Largs, in 1892. He also invented a new compass that was adopted by all British Navy vessels. He worked with Glasgow instrument worker, James White, producing a new range of precise electrical instruments. Kelvin accumulated great wealth through his patents, and published more than 300 papers on aspects of physical science.

Kelvin died at his house near Largs, in 1907. A true scientific innovator, he is buried in Westminster Abbey. His brother, James, was Professor of Engineering at Queen's College from 1857 to 1873 and at Glasgow University from 1873 to his death in 1892. He was also an inventor, patenting his invention for an inward-flow vortex turbine. Their mother, who died in 1830, is buried in Clifton Street Graveyard.

ISABELLA TOD (1836–96) | Suffragette and Campaigner for Women's Education

Isabella Maria Susan Tod was one of the early pioneers of the suffragette movement, lobbying for women's rights in the 19th century. She was born in Edinburgh in 1836 of Scots-Irish parentage but was brought up in Belfast and educated privately. She began her campaigning by contributing to *The Dublin University Magazine* and *The Banner of Ulster*, on the subject of women's rights.

In 1867, she founded the Belfast Ladies' Institute which provided training and courses for women and campaigned for better educational opportunites. She also campaigned for votes for women and was Secretary of the Northern Irish branch of the National Society for Women's Suffrage, established in 1871. Tod was an activist, but she worked mainly through public lectures and petitions. She worked in the Temperance Movement, and also formed a society with Caroline Norton that agitated for changes in the law. This culminated in the Married Women's Property Bill. She was very active with the Ladies National Association, led by Josephine Butler, campaigning against the squalor and disease prevalent amongst prostitutes. She was also involved in the Women's Liberal Unionist Association and was an opponent of Home Rule.

Tod was a supporter of women's higher education and petitioned Queen's College to allow girls to take university honours courses and examinations. The College agreed to admit girls to take tests, although they were awarded certificates rather than degrees. In 1898 a memorial scholarship was set up in her name at Queen's to award distinguished students.

She lived at Claremont Street off the Lisburn Road and later at College Park East, behind Queen's. She is buried at Balmoral Cemetery.

JOSEPH TOMELTY *(1911–95)* | Actor, Novelist and Playwright

Born in Portaferry, Co. Down in 1911, Joseph Tomelty was to influence many spheres of the local arts scene. Moving to Belfast as a young man, he became involved with the St Peter's Players. The drama group developed to become the Northern Ireland Players, which in turn proved the impetus for the Group Theatre in Bedford Street.

As the Group Theatre became established, Tomelty trod the boards and also became its General Manager from 1942 to 1951. At the same time, he was working at the BBC, writing and acting in the local soap opera *The McCooeys*, which ran from 1948 until 1954. Several well-known local actors played in the drama, not least JAMES YOUNG, who built up a following as Derek the Window Cleaner.

In 1951, the theatre director Tyrone Guthrie offered Tomelty a part in the play *The Passing Day*. He proved a great success and this led to character roles in films like *Odd Man Out* and the Hollywood classic *Moby Dick*.

Tomelty wrote a series of acclaimed plays, including the comedies *Barnum was Right* and *Right Again, Barnum*. A more serious play was *All Souls Night*, set on the Ards peninsula amongst fishermen and told in Tomelty's homespun style, combining ingredients of socialist idealism and elitism.

A man of many parts, Tomelty also wrote two novels, *Red is the Portlight*, a rather gloomy tale about seafaring, and *The Apprentice*, set in post-war working-class Belfast against a backdrop of trade unionism, socialism and issues of religion.

At the very height of his success, Tomelty was seriously injured in a car crash while filming *Bhowani Junction* in 1951. He regained consciousness, but tragically was never able to fulfil full-time commitments after the accident.

In 1956, Queen's University awarded Tomelty a Masters for services to the theatre and in 1991, the Arts Council commissioned a bronze bust of this talented local man of letters. On 4th June 1995, Tomelty died at his home in Andersonstown. He was survived by his wife and daughters, Roma and Frances, who have both achieved considerable acting success.

HELEN WADDELL *(1889–1965)* | Scholar and writer

Academic and writer Helen Waddell was born in Tokyo. Her family came from Co. Down, and her father worked as a missionary of the Irish Presbyterian Church, first in Manchuria and later in Japan. Helen showed an early inclination for learning, speaking Japanese and Chinese at a young age. When the family returned to Ireland, they settled in Belfast, and Helen studied at Victoria College in Lower Crescent (see MARGARET BYERS).

Waddell started reading Mathematics at Queen's University, but switched to English in her second year. She gained a First in her B.A. in 1911, and won the ISABELLA TOD Memorial Scholarship for her M.A. thesis on Milton before continuing her studies at Somerville College, Oxford. She worked at the Bodleian Library for several years and later lectured at Bedford College, London.

It is, however, as a writer that Helen Waddell is best remembered. Her first published book was *Lyrics from the Chinese* (1915). Her other works included *Wandering Scholars* (1927), *Medieval Latin Lyrics* (1929) and *The Desert Fathers* (1936). Waddell's first drama, *The Spoilt Buddha*, was performed at Belfast's Grand Opera House by the Ulster Literary Society in 1915.

Her novel *Peter Abelard* was published in 1933. Based on a mediaeval story, it tells the tale of the greatest scholar of his age and his love for convent-girl Heloise. The story is a philosophical slant on both worldly society and the church, and the tension that exists between them. Waddell interpreted the tale using accessible language, without losing the essence of the plot and setting. It has been translated into many languages and has run to over 30 editions.

Waddell was steeped in London literary life. She was Assistant Editor of the magazine *Nineteenth Century* and Vice President of the Irish Literary Society in London, where she included W.B. Yeats, Siegfried Sassoon and Max Beerbohm among her friends. She contributed many articles to *The Standard*, the *Manchester Guardian* and *The Nation*. She was a regular broadcaster and lecturer, and a member of the Irish Academy of Letters. She was the only woman to have won the A.C. Benson medal of the Royal Society of Literature, and was awarded several honorary degrees.

Waddell died in London. She is buried in Magheragally Churchyard, Co. Down.

WILLIAM WALKER *(1871–1918)* | Leader of the Independent Labour Party

A committed socialist, William Walker was the self-educated leader of the Independent Labour Party in Belfast in the early 20th century. His blend of Unionism and Socialism was known as 'Walkerism'.

Born in 1871, Walker initially got involved in Trade Union work at a grass roots level. He organised the Carpenters' and Joiners' Union and gained prominence on the Trades Council. He also worked to improve the lot of textile workers, and in 1898 was elected Poor Law Guardian. As leader of the Independent Labour Party he was often seen addressing crowds at the Custom House steps.

Walker stood in many elections, but for all his hard work, he wasn't very successful. Protestant Trade Unionists rallied to the cause of the Conservatives, especially as the spectre of Home Rule loomed. Walker also fell foul of Dublin activist James Connolly (who was briefly resident in Belfast at 420 Falls Road between 1910 and 1914), due to his Unionist sympathies. The two had a famous, if heated, debate in Belfast. Their argument was prolonged in the press, through the letter pages of a Glasgow newspaper, *Forward*.

In 1904 Walker was elected as a City Councillor and as President of the Irish Trade Union Congress. He was unsuccessful in the elections of 1905, 1906, 1907 and 1910. He lost support in the 1905 by-election, due in no small part to his endorsement of an anti-Catholic questionnaire.

In 1912, he was appointed Inspector of the National Insurance Scheme in the North East. He died in 1918.

ERNEST WALTON *(1903–95)* | Nuclear Scientist and Nobel Prize Laureate

Professor E.T.S. Walton is the only Irish-born scientist to win a scientific Nobel Prize. Born in Dungarvan, Co. Waterford, Walton was the son of a Methodist minister who later moved north. Ernest was educated at Methodist College, Belfast ('Methody') from 1915 to 1922, where he was Head Boy – his future wife, Freda Wilson from Castlereagh, was Head Girl in the same year. Excellent results at Methody took Walton to Trinity College, Dublin, where he attained a Double First in Mathematics and Experimental Science in 1926.

An ensuing scholarship took him to Cambridge University, where he collaborated with John Cockcroft in building a linear accelerator which could accelerate protons to energies of 700,000 electron volts. With this apparatus, they 'split the atom' in 1932.

In 1934, Walton received a fellowship from Trinity College, Dublin, and in 1946 he was appointed as a Professor; a position he held until 1974. Walton's further experiments verified Einstein's Theory of Relativity. The apparatus used (now housed in the British Museum) was primitive, making this landmark in Physics even more laudable. In 1951, Walton and Cockcroft

Professor Ernest Walton, just after winning the Nobel Prize for Physics, 1951

jointly received the Nobel Prize for Physics for their ground-breaking endeavours.

Interestingly, Walton had been pressed to join an unidentified military project in 1944, but Trinity refused to release him. It emerged later as the Manhattan Project to develop the nuclear bomb. Walton, a man of deep religious convictions, was relieved not to have been involved.

Walton had a reputation as an excellent tutor, and made every effort to help his students. He retired in 1974, but continued to work in the Physics Department of the University before moving back to Belfast in 1993. The previous year, Methody – where he was on the Board of Governors for many years – named its new science and technology building in his honour; a fine bronze bas relief of Walton, showing the famous energy equation, was erected on the Walton Building. Walton died in Belfast on 25th June 1995. Predeceased by his wife, he left two sons and three daughters.

SIR WILLIAM WHITLA *(1851–1933)* | Medical Professor and Benefactor

Sir William Whitla was one of Belfast's most important and influential medical figures. Born on 15th September 1851 in Monaghan, he was educated at the Model School there and afterwards apprenticed to Wheeler and Whitaker Chemists in Belfast.

In 1870 he enrolled at Queen's College to study Medicine. He qualified with a First Class Honours degree in 1877, winning the Gold Medal Award. Whitla became a physician to the Belfast Royal Hospital, later the Royal Victoria Hospital, the Belfast Opthalmic Hospital and the Belfast Hospital for Women and Children. He later set up in successful private practice.

Whitla was elected Professor of Materia Medica at Queen's in 1890, and held the position until 1919. He was knighted in 1902 and appointed Physician to the King in Ireland. He was the first M.P. for Queen's from 1918 until 1923 and was appointed Pro Vice-Chancellor in 1924. He wrote several medical books including, *The Dictionary of Treatment*, in 1891, and *The Manual of the Theory and Practice of Medicine* in 1908.

Whitla bequeathed £10,000 to Methodist College to build its Whitla Hall, and provided Queen's with his house at Lennoxvale – where he had lived in great style – to be used as the Vice Chancellor's residence. He had also endowed a Chair of Pharmacology at Queen's, and left money towards the building of the graduation hall there, which was named in his honour. A commemorative bust of him by Gilbert Bayes is set into its west wall, facing onto University Road.

Portrait of Professor Sir William Whitla, Professor of Materia Medica, Queen's College, Belfast, by Frank McKelvey

He was married to Ada Bourne from Stafford, who, in contrast to her husband who was fond of wearing regalia and decorations, once wore her smart but austere Salvation Army uniform to a reception at Buckingham Palace. Prior to living at Lennoxvale, the Whitlas lived at 8 College Square North – in a fine terrace of four-storey houses built c. 1830; No. 8 was destroyed by a bomb in 1977. This street was once known as 'Belfast's Harley Street' due to the large number of doctors who lived and practised there. From 1890 to 1910 many residents moved away due to the overpowering presence of the Technical College, which was built opposite the terrace in the grounds of 'Inst'. Sir William Whitla died after a long illness on 11th December 1933 in Belfast.

GUSTAV WOLFF *(1834–1913)* | Shipbuilder

In partnership with EDWARD HARLAND, Gustav Wilhelm Wolff controlled the biggest shipbuilding concern in the world. He was born in Hamburg in 1834. He was the nephew of Gustav Schwabe, who left Germany for Liverpool, where he became a partner in Liverpool Shipping Company, John Bibby and Sons.

Wolff left Hamburg aged 14, going to live with his uncle in Liverpool. He went to Liverpool College and was then apprenticed to an engineering firm in Liverpool. In 1857 he got a job in Belfast as assistant to Edward Harland, who was then manager of Hickson's shipyard. On 11th April 1861, Harland and Wolff went into partnership together after Harland acquired Hickson's lease. Wolff was able to offer his engineering skills and financial expertise, as well as the link with Bibby in Liverpool that was already paying dividends. The shipyard expanded throughout the 1860s under Harland and Wolff's control. Steamers were built regularly, and the period 1862–64 was particularly lucrative.

In 1873 Wolff became a partner in the Belfast Ropework Company. He became increasingly involved in the ropeworks, especially as the shipbuilding partnership had expanded to include WILLIAM PIRRIE. The ropeworks was able to provide rope and sail cloth to the shipyards at a discount. By 1900 it was the largest in the world.

Wolff was a good humoured man (his personality a perfect foil for Harland's terseness), who settled well in Belfast. He lived in Strandtown and called his house 'The Den'. In 1875, Wolff withdrew slightly from the shipping business, becoming a junior partner. Due to the advantages of success of the early 1880s, he became even less involved in the running of the business, but maintained an interest through regular loans to the firm. In 1892 he entered Parliament after a by-election in East Belfast, as a Conservative; he was nicknamed 'Teutonic' in the House of Commons. He served as an M.P. for 18 years. He returned to the business in the late 1890s, mainly on the financial side, after Harland's death and when Pirrie was Mayor.

In 1903 Gustav Wolff retired, selling his shareholdings to Pirrie who had become somewhat dictatorial in his business dealings. Wolff died in Belfast on 17th April 1913.

JAMES YOUNG *(1918–74)* | Entertainer

Born in Ballymoney, James (Jimmy) Young's family moved to Fernwood Street off the Ormeau Road in South Belfast when Jimmy was six months old. His father looked after the carthorses kept by the Inglis Bakery. After attending Cook Church School, Young got a job in an estate agent's, but his heart always lay elsewhere.

He joined an amateur dramatic group of the Youth Hostel Association at 16, and picked up the Best Actor Award at the Ulster Drama Festival in 1943. Before long, Young was a professional actor, off on whirlwind tours to such diverse venues as Stockport, the West End and the Middle East, where he met lifelong partner, fellow actor and co-scripter Jack Hudson.

Prior to this frenetic schedule, Young met JOSEPH TOMELTY, the local playwright, who cast him in *Right Again, Barnum* at Belfast's Group Theatre. When Young returned home from tour, Tomelty offered him the role of Derek the Window Cleaner in the highly popular radio soap *The McCooeys*.

As a result, Young was invited to go on the road as a variety performer, which helped him increase his experience and earn handsomely at the same time. BBC Radio engaged him with a show called *The Young Idea* in which he played characters like Mrs O'Condriac, Wee Ernie the Shipyard Worker and the Cherryvalley Snob, who all later appeared on television.

In 1960 Young played in local writer Sam Cree's *Wedding Fever* at the Group Theatre – the play lasted for 11 years, breaking all Irish entertainment records. Some of the proceeds went to build the new Arts Theatre in Botanic Avenue. By the mid-1960s, Young was often on

Jimmy Young as Billy Hulk

the road with his solo shows. A new play called *Sticks and Stones* pushed him towards political satire. Simultaneously, his recording career took off as he lampooned every aspect of local life to great effect.

The Troubles forced Young to take another tack. When the Group Theatre closed in 1971 (it has since re-opened), he took his show around the province, entertaining in clubs, bars and town halls; he also toured Canada and the United States. In 1973, the BBC gave him a Saturday night comedy/variety show, featuring *The Young Idea* characters as well as a wide range of others such as Orange Lil, and the Trade Union leader Billy Hulk. His catch-phrases like 'Och, go on' and 'Stap fightin'', which always closed his TV show, wove their way into the popular consciousness. His inimitable comic talent seemed to transcend age, class and religion.

Young was at the height of his career in his mid fifties, working harder than ever – in 1973 worldwide sales of his records exceeded 250,000. Sadly he ignored warnings about his health and died in 1974. His funeral at Roselawn Cemetery was attended by many famous figures from theatre, TV, cabaret and broadcasting.

ROBERT MAGILL YOUNG *(1851–1925)* | Architect and Historian

Robert Magill Young was an architect in Belfast at a time of great development and change in the town's structure. He was also a writer of renown. Young's father, Robert, had worked with SIR CHARLES LANYON and William Dargan. Robert Young was also interested in the arts and Archaeology, and Robert Magill Young followed in his father's footsteps. Magill was Robert's mother's maiden name.

Young senior had established the architecture practice of Young & MacKenzie, which was responsible for the fine Gothic Lennoxvale House, for example, built originally for John Ward of the publishing firm of Marcus Ward and Company and later bought by SIR WILLIAM WHITLA. The company also built up a name as the leading Presbyterian church architects. Whilst Robert Magill Young continued this trend, he also widened the practice's scope in the latter part of the 19th century.

Robert Magill Young was born in Athlone on 6th March 1851 and educated at Dr Reddy's School in Donegall Sqaure, Belfast and at Queen's College. Once qualified, he was involved in building Townsend Street Presbyterian Church and adding to Belmont Presbyterian Church. In 1900, he was involved in a controversy over the new Fisherwick Presbyterian Church on the Malone Road. An initial financial ceiling of £30,000 had to be ditched, and the eventual cost was £70,000. A young architect called Savage was to get the job, but eventually the church authorities appointed Young & MacKenzie.

As Donegall Square developed, Young's company contributed much to its construction, building the Scottish Provident Building, Robinson and Cleaver's department store and the Ocean Buildings; the firm also designed Anderson and McAuley's department store on Donegall Place.

Young also found time to write, and produced an eclectic collection of work which included *A History of the Linen Hall Library*, *A Townbook of Belfast*, *Science as Applied to Industry and Commerce*, *Ulster in '98*, *Historical Notes on Belfast* and even *A Paper on Elk Bones*.

Young lived at 'Rathvarna House' in Chichester Park off the Antrim Road, the family home inherited from his father. Both father and son are buried with other family members in Balmoral Cemetery.

Select Bibliography

Acheson, Alan, *A History of the Church of Ireland 1691–1996*, The Columba Press and APCK, Dublin, 1997

Agnew, Jean, *Belfast Merchant Families in the Seventeenth Century*, Four Courts Press, Dublin, 1996

Bardon, Jonathan, *A History of Ulster*, The Blackstaff Press, Belfast, 1992

Bardon, Jonathan and Burnett, David, *Belfast, A Pocket History*, The Blackstaff Press, Belfast, 1996

Bardon, Jonathan, *Belfast, An Illustrated History*, The Blackstaff Press, Belfast, 1988

Beckett, J.C. et al, *Belfast, The Making of the City 1880–1914*, Appletree Press, Belfast, 1988

Black, Eileen, *Paintings, Sculptures and Bronzes in the Collection of The Belfast Harbour Commissioners*, Belfast Harbour Commissioners, Belfast, 1983

Blackstock, Allan, *Double Traitors? The Belfast Volunteers and Yeomen 1778–1828*, Belfast Society with The Ulster Historical Foundation, Belfast, 2000

Boylan, Henry (ed), *A Dictionary of Irish Biography* (3rd edn), Gill & Macmillan, Dublin, 1999

Brett, C.E.B., *Roger Mulholland – Architect of Belfast*, Ulster Architectural Heritage Society, Belfast

Brodie, Malcolm, *The Tele, A History of the Belfast Telegraph*, The Blackstaff Press, Belfast, 1995

Byrne, Art and McMahon, Sean, *Great Northerners*, Poolbeg, Dublin, 1991

Clarke, Donald (ed), *The Penguin Encyclopedia of Popular Music*, Penguin, London

Clarke, Richard, *The Royal Victoria Hospital, Belfast, A History, 1797–1997*, The Blackstaff Press, Belfast, 1997

Coe, W. E., *The Engineering Industry of the North of Ireland*

Cole, John, *As It Seemed To Me, Political Memoirs*, Phoenix, London, 1995

Collis, John, *Van Morrison, Inarticulate Speech of the Heart*, Little, Brown and

Company, London, 1996

Colgan, Brendan, *Vere Foster: English Gentleman, Irish Champion 1819–1900*, Fountain Publishing, Belfast, 2001

Craig, Patricia, *The Belfast Anthology*, The Blackstaff Press, Belfast, 1999

Cullen Owens, Rosemary, *Smashing Times – A History of the Irish Women's Suffrage Movement, 1889–1922*, Attic Press, 1984

Doherty, Richard and Truesdale, David, *Irish Winners of the Victoria Cross*, Four Courts Press, Dublin, 2000

Duffy, Rita and O' Shea, Suzanne, *Banquet*, Ormeau Baths Gallery, Belfast, 1997

Elliott, Sydney and Flackes, W.D., *Northern Ireland A Political Directory 1968–1999*, The Blackstaff Press, Belfast, 1999

Erskine, J. and Lucy, G., *Varieties of Scottishness*, from Cultural Traditions in Northern Ireland Series, The Institute of Irish Studies, Belfast, 1997

Evans, David and Larmour, Paul, *Queen's, An Architectural Legacy*, The Institute of Irish Studies, Belfast, 1995

Fallon, Brian, *Irish Art 1830–1990*, Appletree Press, Belfast, 1994

Fleming, George, *Magennis VC, The Story of Northern Ireland's Only Winner of the Victoria Cross*, History Ireland, Dublin, 1998

Fletcher, Martin, *Silver Linings, Travels Around Northern Ireland*, Abacus, London, 2001

Galway, James, *James Galway – An Autobiography*, Chappel & Co/Elmtree Books, London, 1978

Garvin, Wilbert and O'Rawe, Des, *Northern Ireland Scientists and Inventors*, The Blackstaff Press, Belfast, 1993

Gleeson, John, *Fyffes Dictionary of Irish Sporting Greats*, Etta Place Publishers, Dublin, 1993

Hamilton, Paul, *Up the Shankill*, The Blackstaff Press, Belfast, 1979

Hill, Myrtle and Pollock, Vivienne, *Women of Ireland, Image and Experience, c.1880–1920*, The Blackstaff Press, Belfast, 1993

Holmes, Finlay, *Our Presbyterian Heritage*, Publications Committee of the Presbyterian Church in Ireland, 1985

Hooks, Mike, *Shorts Aircraft*, The Chalford Publishing Company, Chalford, 1995

Ireland Yearbook, The, Paintings from the Ulster Museum, 1995, 1996, 1997, 2000, 2001, Appletree Press, Belfast, 1995, 1996, 1997, 2000, 2001

Jordan, Alison, *Margaret Byers, Pioneer of Women's Education and Founder of Victoria College, Belfast*, The Institute of Irish Studies, Belfast, 1998

Kennedy, S. B., *Paul Henry*, Yale University Press, London, 2000

Killen, John, *A History of the Linen Hall Library*, Linen Hall Library, Belfast, 1990

Larmour, Paul, *Belfast, An Illustrated Architectural Guide*, Friar's Bush Press, Belfast, 1987

Magee, Jack, *Barney: Bernard Hughes of Belfast 1808–1878*, Ulster Historical Foundation, Belfast, 2001

Maguire, E., *The Sirocco Story*, Belfast Association of Engineering, Belfast, 1954

Maguire, W.A., *Belfast – A History*, Ryburn Publishing/Keele Univeristy Press, Keele, 1993

McCamley, *Belfast Royal Academy, The Second Century, 1885–1985*, W&G Baird, Belfast, 1985

McCavitt, John, *Sir Arthur Chichester, Lord Deputy of Ireland, 1605–16*, The Institute of Irish Studies, Belfast, 1998

McConkey, Kenneth, *Sir John Lavery*, Canongate Press, Edinburgh

Munter, Robert, *Dictionary of Print Trade in Ireland 1550–1775*, Fordham University Press, New York, 1988

Newmann, Kate, *Dictionary of Ulster Biography*, The Institute of Irish Studies, Belfast, 1993

O'Brien, G.O. and Roebuck, P. (eds), *Nine Ulster Lives*, Ulster Historical Foundation, Belfast, 1992

O'Brien, Barry, R., *The Life of Lord Russell of Killowen*, Smith Elder & Co

O'Ceirin, Kit and O'Ceirin, Cyril, *Women of Ireland*, Tir Eolas, Colin Smythe Ltd, Gerrard's Cross

Ormsby, Frank (ed), *The Collected Poems of John Hewitt*, The Blackstaff Press, Belfast, 1991

Owen, D. J., *A History of Belfast*, W & G Baird, Belfast

Peters, Mary and Wooldridge, Ian, *Mary P. Autobiography*, Stanley Paul, London, 1974

Rae, John, *Sister Genevieve*, Little, Brown and Company, London, 2001

Stallworthy, John, *Louis MacNeice*, Faber and Faber, London, 1995

Sweetman, Robin and Nimmons, Cecil, *Port of Belfast, 1785–1985*, Belfast Harbour Commissioners, 1985

Templeton, George E. and Weatherall, Norman, *Images of Ireland: South Belfast*, Gill & Macmillan, Dublin, 1998

Walker, Brian Mercer, *Faces of the Past, A Photographic and Literary Record of Ulster Life 1880–1915*, Appletree Press, Belfast, 1974, 1999

Walker, Brian and McCreary, Alf, *Degrees of Excellence, The Story of Queen's, Belfast 1845–1995*, The Institute of Irish Studies, Belfast, 1994

Walker, Brian, *No Mean City*, Friars Bush Press, Belfast, 1983

Wallace, Martin, *Famous Irish Lives*, Appletree Press, Belfast, 1999

Wallace, Martin, *Famous Irish Writers*, Appletree Press, Belfast, 1999

Wallace, W. Stewart (ed), *The MacMillan Dictionary of Canadian Biography*, University of Toronto Press, Toronto, 1969

Wilson, Judith C., *Conor – The Life and Work of an Irish Artist*, The Blackstaff Press, Belfast

Acknowledgements

The publisher wishes to thank Briony Crozier; John Erskine; Gordon Lucy; Councillor Nelson McCausland, Chair of Development (Arts) Sub-Committee; Dr Eamon Phoenix; and Professor Brian Walker for their help in compiling the list of entries; and also Raymond O'Regan for his contribution to and checking of the text.

The publisher also wishes to thank the following for their help in supplying images: Christine Ashfield, Belfast Harbour Commissioners; Lynda Atcheson and Grainne Loughran, BBC NI Archive, Ulster Folk and Transport Museum; The Church of Ireland Press Office; Rita Duffy; Graeme Farrow, Belfast Festival at Queen's; Rev John Gates, Archdiocese of Armagh; Anita Gibney, Wonderland Promotions Ltd; Rosemary Kelly, BBC NI; Marian Magee, Royal Victoria Hospital; Nicola Mawhinney, Victoria College, Belfast; Pat McLean, Ulster Museum; Dame Mary Peters; Helen Purves, Rodney Miller Associates (for Belfast City Council); Mr C.W. Slator; Mrs M.E. Woods and Sandra Woods.

Photographic credits:

© Appletree Press: p53; © Archdiocese of Armagh: p24; © BBC NI: pp12 & cover (George Best), 34, 71 & cover (Ruby Murray), 82 & cover (Sister Genevieve), 90 & cover (James Young); © Belfast City Council: cover (Harland statue), title page, p6; © Belfast Festival at Queen's: pp 30, 38 (Les Wilson), 48, 68, 75; © Belfast Harbour Commissioners: pp21 & cover (Sir Arthur Chichester), 41, 80; © Christopher Hill Photographic/Jill Jennings: cover (Marie Jones); © Church of Ireland: p33; Courtesy of Rita Duffy: p31; Courtesy of Dame Mary Peters: p76; Courtesy of the Royal Victoria Hospital: pp74, 78, 88; Courtesy of Sony Music Ireland: p48 & cover (Brian Kennedy); Photographs reproduced with the kind permission of the Trustees of the National Museums and Galleries of Northern Ireland: pp 25, 32 & cover (John Boyd Dunlop), 42, 43 (© Basil Blackshaw), 58 & cover (Henry Joy McCracken), 59, 79 (© Mrs Connie Slator), 83; Courtesy of Victoria College, Belfast: p17 & cover (Margaret Byers); Courtesy of Mrs M.E. Woods: p87.

The publisher has made all reasonable efforts to contact living citizens included in this book and to ensure the accuracy of the information contained in it. However, notice of any errors of fact will be gratefully received.